ELK GROVE LIBRARY
8962 ELK GROVE BOULEVARD
ELK GROVE, CA 95624

ELK GROVE LIBRARY
8962 ELK GROVE BLVD.
ELK GROVE, CA 95624

GUTENBERG

Also by John Man

The Waorani: Jungle Nomads of Ecuador
The Atlas of D-Day
Gobi: Tracking the Desert
The Atlas of the Year 1000
Alpha Beta

GUTENBERG

How One Man Remade
the World with Words

John Man

John Wiley & Sons, Inc.

For Dushka

Copyright © 2002 by John Man. All rights reserved

Published by John Wiley & Sons, Inc., New York

First published in Great Britain with the title *The Gutenberg Revolution: The Story of a Genius and an Invention That Changed the World* by Headline Book Publishing in 2002

John Man would be happy to hear from readers with their comments on the book at the following email address: johngarnerman@ukonline.co.uk

Map by ML Design

Diagram on pp. 128–9 by Hardlines

Designed by Ben Cracknell Studios

Typeset by Letterpart Limited, Reigate, Surrey

No part of this publication may be reproduced, stored in a retrieval system, or transmitted in any form or by any means, electronic, mechanical, photocopying, recording, scanning, or otherwise, except as permitted under Section 107 or 108 of the 1976 United States Copyright Act, without either the prior written permission of the Publisher, or authoriza tion through payment of the appropriate per-copy fee to the Copyright Clearance Center, 222 Rosewood Drive, Danvers, MA 01923, (978) 750-8400, fax (978) 750-4744. Requests to the Publisher for permission should be addressed to the Permissions Department, John Wiley & Sons, Inc., 605 Third Avenue, New York, NY 10158-0012, (212) 850-6011, fax (212) 850-6008, email: PERMREQ@WILEY.COM.

This publication is designed to provide accurate and authoritative information in regard to the subject matter covered. It is sold with the understanding that the publisher is not engaged in rendering professional services. If professional advice or other expert assistance is required, the services of a competent professional person should be sought.

ISBN 0-471-21823-5

Printed in the United States of America

10 9 8 7 6 5 4 3 2 1

Contents

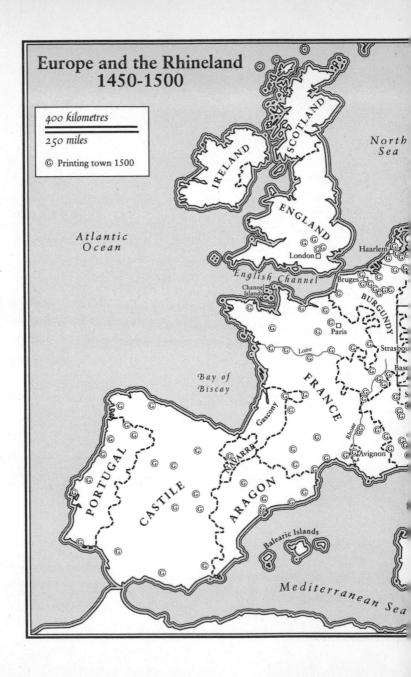

Europe and the Rhineland
1450-1500

400 kilometres

250 miles

Ⓖ Printing town 1500

North Sea

Atlantic Ocean

IRELAND

SCOTLAND

ENGLAND

London

Haarlem

English Channel

Bruges

Channel Islands

BURGUNDY

Paris

Strasbou

Loire

Basc

Bay of Biscay

FRANCE

Gascony

Rhone

Avignon

PORTUGAL

CASTILE

NAVARRE

ARAGON

Balearic Islands

Mediterranean Sea

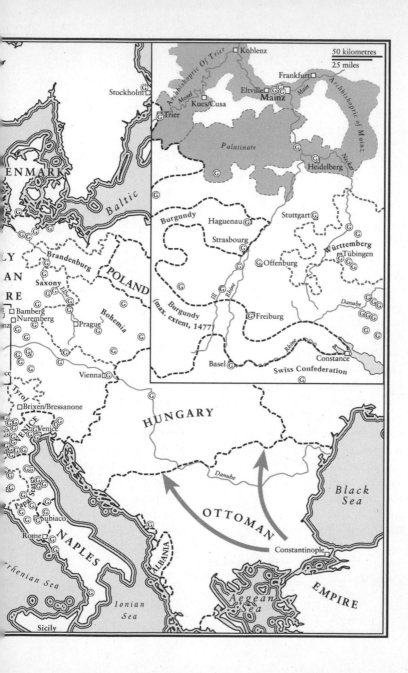

A note on typefaces

An expert eye will notice that this book uses three typefaces. It is my fault for wanting something that suggested a flavour of early printing. The first typefaces were the Germanic, Gothic-style, black-letter texturas, which were hard to read for lay-people then and almost illegible in these secular times. They were replaced in Italy, and then everywhere else outside Germany, by styles derived from Roman inscriptions and Carolingian hand-writing. One of these styles was cut especially for the extraordinary work mentioned in Chapter 9, *Hypnerotomachia Poliphili*. The typeface was revived in the 1920s and named Poliphilus, which gave me the chance to use a digitised version for this book (Poliphilus 12/14: 12-point typesize, 14-point spacing). But my desire for a period feel was achieved at the expense of strict typographical unity. When Poliphilus was originally devised, there was not much variety of typeface: no italics, no bolds, no small capitals (the first Italic was cut in 1500, one year after *HP* appeared). *The Italic Poliphilus used here, known as Blado, was devised on a sixteenth-century model along with the latter-day Poliphilus.* Blado, which exists only in Italic, has no bold, nor a Roman bold equivalent. Nor does Poliphilus. So for both the Roman and Italic bold we opted for Bembo, **which comes from the *same stable as Poliphilus*.**

The Third Revolution

On a graph of human contact over the last 5,000 years, the line from rock-art to e-mail is not a regular curve. It has four turning-points, each recording moments at which written communication flicked to a new level of speed and outreach. The first was the invention of writing itself, which allowed for the creation of big, enduring societies, with priestly elites. The second was the invention of the alphabet, which brought writing within the reach of ordinary people. The fourth, which seems to be turning us into cells in a planet-sized brain, is the coming of the Internet.

This book is about the third turning-point, caused by the invention of printing with movable type, which burst on Europe, and then the world, 550 years ago. Printing changed things so utterly that it is hard to imagine a world without it. In fact, doing so is a futile exercise, because it would have happened anyway. All the elements needed were present across Europe in the fifteenth century – not just in

Germany or in Gutenberg's home town. What Gutenberg provided was that spark that fused these elements into a novelty. It was an invention waiting to happen.

The result, of course, was a new world of communication. Suddenly, in a historical eye-blink, scribes were redundant. One year, it took a month or two to produce a single copy of a book; the next, you could have 500 copies in a week (500 was an average print run in the early days). Distribution was still by foot or hoof, but that didn't matter. A copied book just sits there, waiting for readers, one by one; a successful printed book is a stone dropped in water, its message rippling outwards to hundreds, thousands, millions.

Hardly an aspect of life remained untouched. If rulers could bind their subjects better, with taxes and standardised laws, subjects now had a lever with which to organise revolts. Scholars could compare findings, stand on each other's shoulders and make better and faster sense of the universe. Gutenberg's invention made the soil from which sprang modern history, science, popular literature, the emergence of the nation-state, so much of everything by which we define modernity.

To see a little of what Gutenberg's invention led to, take a look inside Hall 9 at the Frankfurt Book Fair. Hall 9 is the international one, where you will find the American and English publishers and several thousand others from over 100 countries doing their best to express or inspire interest in 400,000 titles, all created since the previous fair. For tyro publishers, the sight of so much *Wurst*, coffee, beer and book-jackets is humbling. Authors should keep their illusions and steer clear.

Here is a former publishing MD, Nick Webb, who previously ran the on-line agency rightscentre.com, surfeited on Hall 9:

Wheelbarrow Decoration, Deathbed Visions, Realising the Inner Self, books on dinosaurs (still), *Vocational Diseases of Professional Cooks, The Semiotics of Sneaker Design*, novels too numerous to mention (at least 20,000 of them fresh new voices), anthropomorphic cutesie-pie animal character series (known as 'merch'), pop-ups, flash-card packs, books with music chips, more bloody dinosaurs, *Die-Cast Models from 1945 to 1948, The Corrs* (in twelve languages), *How to be a Millionaire and Remain a Nice Person, How to be a Millionaire by Being a Complete Bastard, The Legacy of the Biro*, more novels, many written by pretty teenagers who've lived on Ecstasy and Mars bars and are thus highly promotable, *Crime Control Strategies in the Modern Mall, The Art of the Afghani Truck, The Art of the Afghani Truck Vol. 2 – The Golden Period,*

3

Parmenides — the Rediscovered Genius, Was God a Chair-Leg?, The Pre-Socratics Excluding Parmenides, yet more novels from older authors 'at the height of their powers', *Salads with Edible Flowers, Porn, Porn with Marmite* . . . There is no subject so esoteric, daft, narrow or embarrassing that it does not wearily sustain a book or ten. Oh, yes, a few will be sublime expressions of mankind's creative genius that will enrich the reader and culture. But God's teeth, you could heap the remainder into a veritable Alp of dross.

And that is just a single year of English-language titles alone, drawn only from those who make it to Hall 9. There are ten halls at the Frankfurt Book Fair, and a dozen other annual book fairs throughout the world. For a previous book on that earlier invention, the alphabet, I worked out the annual weight of published material. In 1455 all Europe's printed books could have been carried in a single wagon. Fifty years later, the titles ran to tens of thousands, the individual volumes to millions. Today, books pour off presses at the rate of 10,000 million *a year*. That's some 50 million tonnes of paper. Add in 8,000 to 9,000 daily newspapers, and the Sundays, and the magazines, and the figure rises to 130 million tonnes.

This is mountainous. It would make a pile 700 metres high — four times the height of the Great Pyramid. Multiply this by the half-millennium of book publishing since Gutenberg's time, and you have a small mountain range of printed matter. Since most of the increase came in the last century, we could restrict the height of the peaks, but that still leaves us with a hundred pyramids, each of them twice the height of the Great Pyramid. And it goes on: a few years ago it was fashionable to predict the end of the book, but e-publishing has had no impact on the real thing. Ahead lie more and higher peaks of paper.

For historians, the study of this revolution has become an industry, sustaining university departments and museums and researchers and exhibitions and conferences in dozens of cities. The year 2000, supposedly the six-hundredth anniversary of Gutenberg's birth, inspired an international *Fest*. In the British Library, Gutenberg was the 'man of the millennium', as he was, naturally enough, in his home town of Mainz. But everyone wants a share of Gutenberg. Louisville, Kentucky, has no place in the history of printing, but it insisted on its own Gutenberg exhibition solely because it happens to be twinned with Mainz. Keio University in Japan has taken upon itself to gather all examples of Gutenberg's greatest work – his Bible – in digital form (the first results are on show in the British Library, revealing individual letters in microscopic detail). Every year, the Gutenberg Society in Mainz produces a collection of learned papers picking over minutiae of the life and the invention.

Yet at the heart of all this Gutenbergiana there still lie mysteries to be explored and stories to be told, in part because the Gutenberg Bible, like all revolutionary books, acts like a spotlight on our historical eyes: the very act of enlightenment blinds us to its origins. From our standpoint, Gutenberg's Bible looks like a brilliant beginning. But it was also a culmination of two decades of intense research and development, inspired by a vision rooted in the past. Dazzled by the light, we lose sight of the act of creation, and some fundamental questions: Why Gutenberg? Why the Rhineland in particular? Why the mid-fifteenth century? How might things have been different if it had been someone else, somewhere else, at another time? To get to the heart of the matter, how did he actually come to the idea? How much was down to his personal genius?

To explore these questions means entering an alien world, stepping back into the past across the bridge provided by Gutenberg's invention. In Gutenberg's time, Europe was an empty continent, compared with today. Towns were no larger than modern villages, linked only by unpaved tracks. In western Germany it took half a day, on average, to walk or ride from one to the next, through forests that were the domains of wolves and spirits. At night, if you were foolish or unlucky enough to be out in the countryside, you would see no artificial glimmer to lighten clouded skies or rival the stars. Large buildings – cathedrals, or castles, or monasteries – were wonders for ordinary people, who lived with the seasons, at the mercy of disease, climate and warring rulers. Even an educated person had only the vaguest idea of events that would define eras for later generations. Experimental science was an impossibility, the Christian God a living presence, immortal souls as real as bodies, and sin as foul as plague. In pursuit of salvation, pilgrims by the ten-thousand toured hundreds of holy places, in lieu of undertaking a hazardous, year-long journey to the Holy Land itself. For a small fee, one could buy an indulgence, which freed one from the burden of sin for a time. These conditions and attitudes were set in a long-gone context, the seething patchwork of tiny units that formed the German-speaking world, the Holy Roman Empire, from which Germany would not emerge for another 400 years.

※ ※ ※

Researching these questions led me to conclusions that surprised me.

If printing was one of the foundations for the modern world, then – I had supposed – Gutenberg had to be a selfless genius, in the vanguard of modernity, dedicated to improving the world, eager to bring to it the benefits of new knowledge.

Not a bit. The truth, it now seems to me, is the precise

opposite of my preconceptions. Gutenberg's aim, I believe, was that of a businessman striving to be the first to cash in on the Continent-wide market offered by the Catholic Church. It was as an early capitalist that he was a modernist. But that aim could be fulfilled only if he could do something thoroughly reactionary, and unify a divided Christendom. It is one of history's greater ironies that he achieved exactly the reverse of his intentions. Having succeeded at last, with an astounding display of brilliance and perseverance, he almost lost everything to his partners and colleagues, only by the skin of his teeth avoiding poverty and obscurity. And having produced one of the greatest of Christian publications, he ushered in a revolu-tion – the Reformation – that blew Christian unity apart for ever.

His story is one of genius very nearly denied. A few records less, and we would not now be revering the Gutenberg Bible as his. All we would have would be the results: an idea that changed the world, and a book that is among the most astonishing objects ever created, a jewel of art and technology, one that emerged fully formed, of a perfection beyond any-thing required by its purpose. It is a reminder that the business Gutenberg started does indeed contain elements of the sub-lime – that at the heart of the mountains of printed dross there is gold.

CHAPTER 1

A Golden City, Tarnished

Coming to Mainz in around 1400, you have the best view if you approach along the Rhine. Let's say that you are travelling upstream, as the Gutenberg family often did from their estate ten kilometres to the north. The ferryman and his gang of eight rowers hug the river bank to avoid the mid-stream current. Ahead, where the inflow of the Main lays a tongue of silt, the boat turns to make the crossing. You see the city, a collection of spires and roofs parcelled by a wall. You edge past three hulking milling-ships, waterwheels churning slowly in the current, and approach a clutter of wharves where a dozen ships are docked. Others lie moored in a backwater, awaiting cargoes. Two floating cranes swing bales of cloth on to the foreshore, which slopes 100 metres up to the city wall. Closer up, the wall resolves into house-ends and bastions broken by four gated towers, through which drayhorses haul their carts. Beyond the wall is a silhouette of

9

wooden-tiled roofs and a hedgehog of spires – forty, actually, if you care to count them. From them comes the first sound of the city, the clang of bells. Over all looms a sturdy tower of dark-red sandstone, the steeple of St Martin's Cathedral, the centrepiece of the city that still glories in its Roman name: *Aurea Maguntia*, Golden Mainz.

As you approach, the woodcut charm fades, and the smell hits. The foreshore is a mess of mud and horses, across which you pick your way towards the main gate, the Iron Tower, named after the metalworkers who have offered their wares here for almost 200 years. You pass through outer and inner doors and past guards. Inside, you find turmoil and noise. Barefoot peasants hawk combed flax, fishmongers offer catch straight from the river, traders elbow past with fabrics from Holland and Burgundy, horses vie with cows for street space, pigs and sheep mix with carts and people. The drains are sewage ditches running beside main streets roughly paved with planks: there will be no true paving-stones in Mainz for a century. Alleys are all mud and dung. For a new arrival, it seems chaos. But not for townsmen, who know the hierarchy. You would be lucky to see the ruler, the archbishop and his retinue, making a show of authority in their fancy fabrics; you might miss the sight of a merchant's wife, in scarlet lamb's wool and rabbit-fur trimmings, emerging from one of the stone houses now favoured by the rich over the older, half-timbered ones; but you can't miss the craftsmen, who drive the city's commercial life and turn its streets into pageants.

Like unions in an old-fashioned newspaper business, each craft has its place of work and its members grouped into a guild. At this point in time, there are thirty-four guilds in Mainz, and most of them do work that assaults the senses. Here is the sweet smell of wood-merchants' timbers, a blast of heat from a pot-maker's oven, the scent of new-baked bread, a pungent carpet of sawdust and wood-shavings. Stonemasons and slate-roofers chip and hammer, tanners and leather-workers cure and scrape and cut. Some crafts could be familiar enough – tailors, carpenters, furriers, blacksmiths and vegetable gardeners. Others you scarcely see nowadays: coopers, salt-measurers, warpers, barber-surgeons (they were one and the same profession then). Down other streets are metalworkers, saddlers, painters, vintners, wine-sellers, ropemakers, chestmakers, bucklers, linen-weavers, hedgers, shoemakers and cobblers, all the professions common to any medieval city. Other guilds are special to a river port, like the river pilots and fishermen. But here in Mainz the upriver fishermen do not have identical interests with downriver fishermen, nor the upriver goods forwarders with their downriver counterparts. All proclaim their expertise and pride with coats of arms, which decorate clothing, goods and houses like tribal totems. New arrivals soon learn to recognise the stag salient of the Upper Lane butchers, the ox passant of their Lower Lane colleagues and rivals.

Threading your way through this messy throng, along streets that still bear the same names today, you cross the marketplace, past the booths of the forty-eight licensed cloth-sellers and past the cathedral, where work is just starting on two-storey cloisters. To your right, behind the mint, is the town hall, with its crenellated gable. Squeeze between this and the rectangular façade of the Staple Hall, where river traders have to offer their wares, force your way past boy-labourers carting fish and some town official checking a barrel of tallow, follow a few lanes, and you come to a simple, solid church with a stubby three-storey tower that will soon be given a spire marking it as one of the city's landmarks. The church is named after St Christopher, the patron saint of travellers, who in legend carried the Christ-child across a river.

A stone's throw beyond, where the Christophstrasse joins the Schustergasse – Cobblers' Lane – is one of Mainz's solid upper-class houses. It has two wings, joined at an angle, each of three storeys. It has elements of a fortress – not surprising, given Mainz's history of civil strife. Little windows pierce the ground-floor walls, allowing a dim light into the storerooms within. The living quarters are upstairs, which is home for several family members and their close relatives.

You have reached the Gutenberg house.

I might have suggested starting the search today, but it's a mildly depressing experience, thanks to wartime bombs. St Christopher's, one of the few buildings to survive from 1400, is a ruin, its Romanesque walls buttressed by 1960s concrete and floored with weeds. And the original Gutenberg house, after much rebuilding, was totally flattened. Its bland and functional replacement is a pharmacy – Mohren, run by the Mann family. They specialise in medicinal teas. No ghost walks its fragrant back rooms.

❖ ❖ ❖

In 1400 this had been known as the Gutenberg house for over a century, but not because the inventor's family lived here. Unfortunately for us, Gutenberg was the name of the house, not the family, at least not yet. At the time, family names such as we know them today were rare. If an upper-crust, non-aristocrat was known by anything other than a Christian name, it was almost always by the name of his house or estate, *von* this or *zu* that (or *vom*, or *zum* or *zur*, as grammar dictated), or occasionally, in areas bordering France, *de*. Towns, villages, districts and large houses all acted as markers, which stuck to the current owner, as in

'Anne of Green Gables' or 'Toad of Toad Hall'. But there was nothing rigid about this. If a family moved, or bought another house, the house name might go with them for a while, or not, or a new house name might be added. So different families might have the same name, and the same family often changed names or acquired more, which accumulated like silt, generation by generation. It is a system that makes genealogical research in medieval Germany a nightmare.

In our case, we're in luck twice over, because the house name not only leads on to the man, but also back to the heart of his times. Originally, the Gutenberg house was the 'Judenberg', the Jewish Hill, a name with significant connotations. The Jews, scattered across Europe and the Middle East by the Romans, had prospered under Charlemagne 500 years before, forging trade links for this new empire. By 1000 there were some 20,000 of them in fifty towns dotted across Northern Europe. They became the 'Ashkenazim', after the son of Noah's son Gomer, whose language was traditionally equated with German. They had no natural place in feudal Europe, neither owing allegiance to a lord, nor being lords in their own right. Hence their special roles as traders and bankers, increasingly important as Europe's economy became less feudal and more urban. But they lived on a knife edge. In 1096, in the upsurge of xenophobia that marked the opening of the First Crusade, they became targets. Thereafter pogroms occurred every 50 to 100 years. On the one hand they were respected as the people of the Old Testament and officially tolerated by the Church 'in accordance with the clemency that Christian piety imposes' (the words are those of Pope Innocent III in 1199). On the other they could just as easily be despised as Christ-killers, usurers, slave-traders and potential traitors lusting for the pure and innocent blood of Christian children. One rumour – officially denied, widely credited from the thirteenth century on – was that Jews had a habit of acquiring a 'host', the technical term for consecrated bread used in the Communion. By papal decree in 1215, the host magically transubstantiated into Christ's flesh as it was taken into the mouth, in accordance with his instructions at the Last Supper. Having as it were acquired Christ's body, people muttered, the Jews then *damaged* it. By this paranoid reasoning, akin to the belief that witches could work black magic with dolls, Jews became 'Christ-torturers', and subject to several murderous anti-Semitic pogroms.

Mainz was the capital of European Jewry. It had had its own Jewish academy for over 300 years. It was revered as the home of Gershom ben Judah, the 'Light of the Diaspora', who in the eleventh century was the first to bring copies of the Talmud to Western Europe and whose directives (*takkanot*) helped Jews adapt to European practices. There had of course been pogroms – in the 1096 outbreak, 1,300 Jews were killed, and hundreds more expelled or forced to convert to Christianity, a pattern repeated in 1146 and 1282. On each occasion, influential Jews were invited back, families re-formed, the community rebuilt itself. In the mid-fourteenth century, Mainz had the largest Jewish com- munity in Europe: some 6,000.

In the 1282 pogrom, fifty-four Jewish properties were abandoned and were grabbed by the rich and powerful. It seems that the Gutenberg house fell to the archbishop's treasurers, Philipp and Eberhard, who named themselves after their new acquisition: de Gudenberg. It was later acquired by the great-great-grandfather of our inventor and stayed in the family.

This ancestor was named Frilo, who had two houses, one with the unlikely name of Gensfleisch – Goose Flesh. No one knows why. Frilo left historians with two little prob- lems. The first involves his coat of arms, which was used by two family lines, his own and that of his second wife's family, who were named Sorgenloch, probably after a vil- lage sixteen kilometres south-west of Mainz now called Sörgenloch, with an umlaut. The design shows a hooded, stooping figure, bearing some sort of a burden on his back, leaning on a stick and holding out a bowl. He is wearing an odd pointed cap with a bobble, perhaps a bell, attached to its point. First recorded in the late fourteenth century, it comes in several versions; one, rediscovered in 1997 during renovations on the cathedral, was carved in stone as a house-marker. In its most common form, the man is an odd figure, with a severe stoop and a shuffling gait, and the cumbersome something or other on his back is hidden by a cloth. This historical oddity has so puzzled researchers that it has become a sort of inkblot into which they have read immense significance. Was this a mendicant friar, a fool, a pilgrim, a pedlar, a beggar? Was that cloak-covered hump a bundle of goods or a hunchback? Was that odd pointed cap a Jewish hat, like the ones used to identify Jews in medieval Christian art? And why would a patrician family wish to be identified with any of these images?

In fact, the figure may not have originally been quite so peculiar, as one version suggests. This was recorded in Austria for an odd but instructive reason. The Gutenberg house, you will recall, was just next door to St Christopher's, which was being completed at about the time Frilo arrived. In

the 1380s St Christopher inspired a certain Austrian shep-
herd named Heinrich – known as Henry the Foundling – to
build a lodge to help travellers crossing the formidable Arl-
berg Pass from Switzerland into Austria. The local ruler,
Leopold III, a Habsburg, supported the scheme, which
must have seemed a good way to link his western Austrian
domains to his Swiss ones. The new Fraternity of St
Christopher raised funds through branches in many parts
of Germany, including Mainz. What better way for a rising
family to show its generosity and stature than by linking
itself with the patron saint of their local church? Several
members of the Gensfleisch family did just that, promising
a small annual sum and a one-off payment of one gulden
(about two weeks' wages for a master craftsman) when they
died, as the register of the Fraternity records. Beside each
entry is a little Gensfleisch coat of arms with its strange
figure. It is a traveller, heading into a wind, his cloak and
pointed hood flapping over his shoulder. On his back is a
small sack of possessions – not many, for this is a poor man.
His hose is out at the knees, he has simple shoes, not boots,
and he is holding out a bowl for food or alms. There is no
hunchback or heavy concealed burden. He seems quite fit,
a cheery figure striding along into the wind with his
walking-stick.

The surviving copies of the shield, kept in the archives of
St Pölten, west of Vienna, suggest a scenario: the idea for the

coat of arms arises when the family comes to live in the house just next door to St Christopher's. The figure is conceived as a St Christopher, with his Christ-child burden. But something changes the designer's mind, because he is from the family of Frilo's second wife, the Sorgenlochs. Sorgenloch means 'hole of cares'. But the verb '*sorgen*' carries the sense of 'to care for' as well as 'to be burdened with cares', as does 'care' in English. Perhaps what we have here is a figure who carries a complex of meanings – a St Christopher who has mutated into a sort of holy Everyman, wearing the common-or-garden pointed cap, the *Gugelmütze* still to be seen in Mainz festivals, soliciting help in his task of bearing the cares of the world. None of this is backed by evidence, by the way, but it is less wild than some theories, and more charming than most. I like to think this was the Gensfleisch (and Sorgenloch) way of stating their adherence to the Christian virtues of humility and fortitude.

Then there is the second problem left by Frilo. Why did he not add 'Gutenberg' to his list of names? One possibility is that his family had a perfectly sound sense of themselves, with several properties to their credit, and their coat of arms now rooted them firmly in Mainz society. But that seems to me only a partial answer. Eventually, following custom, it would have been natural to name themselves after their new family house. The time might well have come around the middle of the fourteenth century; except that there occurred something so dreadful that it quite put the idea out of mind.

+‡+   +‡+   +‡+

To explain what happened, let us consider for a moment the marmots of Mongolia. These creatures, common on the Central Asian grasslands, are charming to look at and make an excellent stew, but are occasionally better avoided because they are favoured by fleas, which can harbour a virulent bacillus, which kills both fleas and marmots. In the right circumstances, when marmots are few, the fleas may spread to other species – rabbits, rats and eventually humans. Once in the bloodstream, the bacillus causes a reaction that is usually (though not always) fatal. It strikes either the lungs (ninety per cent fatal) or the blood (100 per cent fatal) or, most commonly, the lymph glands. These glands, unable to drain off the poison, balloon into hard, dark, nut-sized swellings known as 'buboes', to which the affliction owes its name – the bubonic plague, better known as the Black Death.

Sometime in the 1340s, the marmots of Mongolia suffered a decline. *Pasteurella pestis* sought other hosts and found them conveniently commuting along the pony-express routes created by the Mongols in their explosive conquests over the preceding 150 years. A few years later, the fleas and their nasty little parasites reached the Crimea. There the local Mongols were besieging the ancient port of Feodosiya, which Italian merchants from Genoa had taken over in the previous century as a 'factory', or trading station, renaming it Kaffa. Stricken by the plague, the Mongols withdrew, with a parting shot. In December 1347 they catapulted the plague-ridden bodies of their own dead over the walls to infest the Italians. The next ship heading back to the Mediterranean carried the plague, in its rats, in its flea-ridden materials and in its crew. From Italy and southern France the plague spread north at an average rate of fifteen kilometres a week, visiting upon Europe its greatest catastrophe ever. In three years something like 25 million people died, perhaps more. A papal inquiry put the figure at 40 million. This represented a third of Europe's population. In some places the death toll may have topped sixty per cent. The devastation was almost universal, and the effects scarred cities, cultures and minds for generations.

Of the causes, no one knew anything at all at the time, and therein lay the true horror. There have been events of equivalent impact – the Holocaust, the Hiroshima and Nagasaki bombs, AIDS when it was first reported – but none of a comparable scale. It is the lack of explanation that unhinges minds. People can cope with fear and suffering better if they understand, or feel they do. In Nazi concentration camps, Communists and Jehovah's Witnesses preserved their sanity in a world gone mad with the certainty that they were players in a drama written by the laws of either history or God. Christian Europe saw only a world turned upside down. The biblical God promised both salvation in the next life and support in this one. Now He seemed suddenly impotent, if not positively antagonistic. Why? Ignorance bred a hysterical rush for explanations and redress. God must be angry at human sin; clearly He was out to impose punishment; so perhaps He could be mollified if humans undertook their own pre-emptive punishment. Across Europe, groups of crazed devotees marched from city to city, lashing themselves with iron-tipped thongs, crying for God's mercy, while onlookers moaned and dabbed clothes in the blood to provide themselves with healing relics.

And who or what had been the cause of God's ire? An answer was close to hand. It was all the fault of the Jews. In Geneva, Jews were tortured until they confessed the truth: *they had poisoned the wells*. To minds broken by ignorance and fear, it all made sense. In the popular mind, the Jews were, after all, Christ-torturers and child-murderers. Across Germany the word spread that the Jews were also 'well-poisoners'. Here was the scapegoat needed to assuage an angry God, and vengeance was swift. On St Valentine's Day 1348, reported the chronicler Jakob Twinger von Königshofen, 'the Jews were burned in Strasbourg in their churchyard on a wooden scaffolding. And anything owed to the Jews was regarded as settled. Any cash owned by the Jews was taken by the council and distributed among the craft trades. Thus it was that the Jews were burned in Strasbourg and in the same year in all the cities along the Rhine.' Arriving in some new town, eager for more blood to feed their frenzy, bands of flagellants headed for the Jewish quarters to root out evil. In Antwerp and Brussels, the entire Jewish community was slain. In Erfurt, 3,000 perished. In Worms and Frankfurt, the Jews, facing certain death, resorted to the tradition of Masada, and committed mass suicide.

In 1348–9 the plague struck Mainz. Some 10,000 people – perhaps half its inhabitants – died. Its citizens sought their traditional scapegoats. Here, in a response that seems to have been unique, the Jews fought back as the mob closed in. They killed 200 people before retreating into their own homes. In vain: on Bartholomew's Day, 24 August, 100 of them were burned outside St Quentin's Church.

For the Church and temporal rulers, this was madness beyond endurance. Flagellants usurped the role of priests, claiming a direct line to God; and if the Jews were killed, who would fund enterprise and war? The Pope recalled the tradition of tolerance and banned the flagellants. Kings and dukes followed suit. The flagellants vanished, in the words of an eyewitness, 'like night phantoms or mocking ghosts', and the surviving Jews again rebuilt their lives.

In Mainz, as everywhere, there was no easy escape from

these dreadful events, for the plague returned twice more in the next decades, reminding all of their helplessness. A city of 20,000 was reduced to a rump of some 6,000 people, the number of guilds dropped from fifty to thirty-four and Golden Mainz found itself with a good deal of its gilt scratched off. But the horrors lived on – in anecdote, in song, in dance, in painting, in sculpture – to the point of obsession. Artists replaced images of soulful serenity with visions of worms and putrefaction. Mainz, like hundreds of towns and villages throughout Europe, had its *danse macabre* (a term of disputed origin, first recorded in 1376). This death-dance reminded participants of the fate that would come to all, high and low. 'Advance, see yourselves in us', chant skeletons in a fourteenth-century mural of a *danse macabre* in the Church of the Innocents in Paris, 'dead, naked, rotten and stinking. So will you be ... Power, honour, riches are naught; at the hour of death only good works count.' Death, the great leveller, opened the dance, summoning people from squares and houses, leading them to the graveyard. There, to raucous tunes, Death's skeletal assistants beckoned the pope, king, queen and cardinal to a ritualised end, followed by ordinary townsfolk and peasants, mocking and mowing in back-to-front breeches with cow-bells tied between their legs and beer-flagons freely passed around, flattening them until Judgement Day bid them arise and stagger home to their beds and hangovers.

And so with these grim realities in mind – a fearful plague, an atrocious act of anti-Semitism – the Gensfleisch family forbore to link themselves to the house on Jews' Hill. Perhaps their association with St Christopher suggested some faint notion that to become Gutenbergs might not be in the best of taste. Better to wait until memories began to fade.

✣✣   ✣✣   ✣✣

The inventor's father, Friele Gensfleisch zur Laden – picking up a house name from another family property – was well off. He inherited a farm, part of the Gutenberg house, and an income from the interest on a loan made by Mainz to the town of Wetzlar in 1382. His position was secured by marriage to a woman of property, Else Wirich. It was she who brought into the family the country estate in Eltville, ten kilometres downriver. Though neither rich nor aristocratic, the family was eminent enough to rank among the worthies of the town, the 100 or so families who referred to themselves as *Geschlechter* (the Families) or *Alten*, 'ancients'. The current term, inherited from nineteenth-century usage which favoured classical connections, is 'patricians'. As a member of the 'patrician' establishment, Friele inherited a position as 'Companion of the Mint', which sounds rather grand, for this key economic body was controlled by the archbishop. In fact, it was more like being a member of an exclusive club, which protected itself by demanding that members should be true-blue patricians back to all four grandparents. He also inherited a right to trade in the cloth that had to be offered for sale by all cloth-merchants passing up and down the Rhine – an upper-class trading monopoly gained in exchange for providing protection from the Rhine's 'robber barons'. It was on his death in 1419 that his heirs decided the time had come to join house name and family, and officially referred to him as Friele Gensfleisch zur Laden *zum Gutenberg*.

By then his son Johann – Gutenberg, as we can now call him – was a young man. How old exactly? No one knows. The only certainty is that, on the evidence of his father's will, he was of age by 1420, which means he was born sometime between 1394 and 1404. The only reason his birthday is supposedly in 1400, and why it seems a good date to begin this book, is purely down to some well-judged public relations by Mainz's city fathers.

What happened was this:

As the significance of Gutenberg's invention in 1440 became ever more obvious, it became the subject of centennial celebrations. In 1540 Wittenberg took the lead, followed a century later in Leipzig, Breslau and Strasbourg. In 1740 Dresden, Bamberg, Halle and Frankfurt joined in. Mainz was slow off the mark. It took the French to point out what they were missing, after Napoleon's army took Mainz in

1792. The revolutionaries knew how to value printing. A Franco-German with the glorious name of Anacharsis Cloots made a passionate speech to the National Assembly, extolling Gutenberg as a benefactor of mankind whose ashes should at once be joined with those of the great and good in the Pantheon in Paris. 'Gutenberg's invention', he cried, 'will become the tool with which we will rework the future!' He was guillotined two years later, but his message had been heard. French administrators in 'Mayence', now the bastion of France's eastern frontier, spent 2 million francs tearing down old buildings to create today's Gutenbergplatz, with its statue staring in scholarly meditation at the theatre opposite. At last, over 300 years after his death, Gutenberg was Mainz's favourite son.

Still, it was the *invention*, not the *man,* that they celebrated. So it continued after France's defeat in 1815. In 1840 Germans struggling to paste together a nation from medieval shards found in printing a fitting symbol of German enter-prise and creativity. In eighty-nine towns from Aachen to Zurich, German-speakers celebrated their discovery in verses, pageants and concerts. Mainz's own two-day festival was rather overshadowed. What Gutenberg's home town really needed was a unique event, something all its own.

In the 1890s the city fathers saw their chance. They would celebrate Gutenberg's *birthday*. No matter that no one knew when it was – uncertainty offered an opportunity. It could be any year they wanted. And what better year than the turn of the century? Paris was planning to cash in on the centennial with a great international festival, which should not go unchallenged. Ideas were mooted, plans proposed. The mayor took matters in hand. He wrote to the leading Gutenberg scholar, Karl Dziatzko of Göttingen, to ask his advice. Back came exactly the right reply: since no one knew precisely when Gutenberg was born, and since everyone agreed it was sometime around the turn of the century, in Dziatzko's opinion one might as well opt for a nice round year, namely 1900, as the time to celebrate Gutenberg's birthday – his five hundredth, no less. And on what day should it be celebrated? Again, since any day could be chosen, Mainz might as well opt for the most suitable – Johann's own name day, the Feast of St John the Baptist, 24 June. Furthermore, nothing less than an international festival would do the occasion justice. And finally it should all revolve around a new society created in Gutenberg's name.

This was music to municipal ears. At a meeting of Mainz's journalists and writers on 20 April 1896, the mayor presented this glorious vision, and the local paper, the *Mainzer Anzeiger*, backed him in ringing tones: 'Everyone agreed that Mainz was not only justified in opting for a festival – it had a duty to do so.' So PR made history. From then on, the world looked to Mainz, where the Gutenberg

Museum became a focal point for Gutenberg studies and Gutenberg tourism. As far as the public is concerned, our hero entered the world on 24 June 1400.

Johann (or Johannes: the spelling varied) was born into Mainz's establishment and baptised, according to unsubstantiated tradition, in St Christopher's. There is no information about his early education, but his later skills suggest that his elderly father and commercially minded mother made sure he had a good start in one of Mainz's several schools. It could have been a church school – St Christopher's had one – but there were others, run by townspeople, where pupils learned to write using the combination of capital and small letters favoured by Church and state bureaucracies. He might have learned the numbering system from Arabian lands, of which traditionalists still disapproved. In any event he would have learned Latin, the language of scholars and churchmen in a continent that was all dialects and no agreed 'national' languages. If he went to the school run by the Carmelite brethren, just beyond St Christopher's, he would have been taught by priests trained in Avignon and Oxford. Committed to Christlike poverty and intellectual rigour, they drilled their pupils until they could chat to each other in Latin. For the first ten years of his life, it must have seemed that little

Johann – Henchen ('Little Hans') as he was known – was in for a contented and secure childhood.

But a number of factors combined against him. His mother, Else Wirich, came from a family who had gone down in the world. A great-grandfather had chosen the wrong side in a small-scale civil war in the early fourteenth century and ended up marrying the daughter of an Italian moneychanger. Their son, Else's father, was a mere shop-keeper. Friele Gensfleisch married beneath himself. Why he did so we will never know. Perhaps it was for love. If so, it was not the first love match to have social consequences. Their children – Johann, his elder brother Friele and sister Else – lacked the background to inherit his father's position as a Companion of the Mint. There would be no easy access to upper-class influence for Henchen.

Anyway, upper-class life in Mainz had its problems. This was a city in deep trouble. Not that an outsider would have seen much cause for concern. The archbishop, Johannes of Nassau (a village forty-eight kilometres to the north-west), commuting between his estate in Eltville and his residence beside the cathedral in Mainz, seemed the very image of stability. Through his people – his chancellor and the mayor – he controlled the 'ancients' – the patricians – in their heredi-tary posts in the town hall, the mint, the law court and the Staple Hall. His income and the cathedral's was assured, from his lands, from the fees for Masses to be said for the dead, from the sale of documents absolving purchasers of their sins (a business of which we will hear a good deal more later).

But insiders knew this show of control was a sham. In the taverns where the guildsmen downed their wine – for every guild had its favourite haunt – the lads drank to their own rising power. Ever since the archbishop had allowed property owners to form a council in the twelfth century, the forty odd seats on the town council had slipped from high born to lower born. In the mid thirteenth century the council men had all been the archbishop's nominees. In 1332, after the two sides came to blows in a nasty little civil war, the archbishop backed off, and patricians and guilds divided the council between them. A century later, in Gutenberg's lifetime, the guildsmen would gain total control. Meanwhile, resentments built, tamped down by regularly revised agreements in which the townsfolk swore allegiance, promised to keep the peace, not to carry weapons, to avoid feuding and so on and so forth in articles that entirely failed to resolve the underlying tensions.

One cause of resentment was the profligacy and selfishness of the patricians. They refused to pay taxes. And they had discovered the joys of capitalism, in the form of annuities. It was a wonderful idea: you paid a lump sum to the city, and the city 'repaid' five per cent of the sum every year for twenty years – and then went on paying, to you if you survived, to your heirs if you didn't. In effect, a loan repayment of five per cent per annum simply became an everlasting interest payment of five per cent. Johann was himself a beneficiary, with two annuities that paid him a total of twenty-three gulden ('golden', the Rhenish equivalent of the Italian gold coin named a 'florin', after its town of origin, Florence).

In the short run the scheme looked good. All the city needed was a flow of initial payments. In the long run, however, the city fathers had to make more than they paid out in interest, as modern insurance companies do. But they couldn't. There was no stock market to play, and they needed the assets to run the town hall, to repair the walls and to employ scribes and lawyers and watchmen. So the only way they could keep up the payments was to get more deposits. They were, in effect, creating a financial pyramid, which depended on ever more capital to keep itself going. By the early fifteenth century interest on the debt was eating up forty per cent of the income from ground rents and taxes, and rising inexorably. Soon there would be no more citizens to contribute. The city would be having to pay 100 per cent of its income in annuities, and there would be no income. The place would be bust. The guildsmen, who neither controlled this system nor benefited from it, objected ever more vociferously.

In the summer of 1411 tempers flared, again. On the council, guildsmen opposed a patrician candidate for mayor. Sixteen leading guildsmen urged their patrician colleagues to loosen up, or else. But loosening up meant revolution. The patricians would have to lose their privileges, pay taxes and abandon their comfortable annuities. The patricians, though, knew what to do, because their grandparents had shown them, back in the civil war of 1332. The rich had simply left town for their country estates until the townsmen felt the pinch of absent money and allowed a return. In that summer of 1411, 117 patricians decamped, most of them with their families. Among them was Friele Gensfleisch and – it's safe to assume – Else, with Johann and his elder brother and sister, making a hasty retreat downriver to Eltville, where the archbishop's castle and retinue offered protection to those lucky enough to own property. There and in other outlying areas the well-off sat tight to await better times.

Better times did not come. Though the archbishop mediated and families returned, the city remained angrily divided between guildsmen and patricians. Friele took his family off to safety again in 1413, this time for an extended stay. In 1415 the German king himself intervened, and Mainz's problems jumped from the local to the national stage.

✢✢ ✢✢ ✢✢

The word 'national', however, is a modern imposition. True, the Germans had a king; but what he ruled, or tried to rule, was not a nation in a modern sense. And true, Germans shared a language and a culture, and referred to themselves as a 'people'; but as a place 'Germany' had no heart and was fuzzy round the edges. Traditionally, Germans thought of themselves as people who lived between the Rivers Rhine and Elbe. In 1400, though, the German people included not only those of today's Austria, but also an ever-increasing area in the east as Germans colonised Hungary, Poland, western Russia, the Baltic states and the Czech-speaking areas of Bohemia. The first German university was founded in Czech-speaking Prague in 1348.

There was no centre driving this outward flow, but rather dozens of centres of different kinds: dukedoms, princedoms, margravates, counties and Church estates, some with bishops who were also princes, some whose bishops were ruled by princes. Every local ruler could hope to make up his own authority and answer to none. As Duke Rudolf IV of Habsburg said: 'I myself intend to be pope, archbishop, bishop, archdeacon and dean in my land.' In 1366 Abbot Mangold of Reichenau on Lake Constance arrested five fishermen for poaching, put their eyes out with his own fingers and sent them home to Constance without fear of reprisal.

Towns (like Mainz) were the wildest cards in this motley pack. Traditionally, rulers swapped, pledged, mort-gaged or sold them. But in 1400, when there were about thirty German towns of over 2,000 people, this was becoming harder, for the townspeople themselves objected, turning their communities into hotbeds of enterprise and ambition and class conflict.

It all amounted to an unruly mess: imagine the Balkans multiplied by ten. In 1400 some 400 entities, all pursuing their own economic and dynastic interests, formed a politi-cal slurry, like a country-sized microscope-slide on which cells shifted and bred and merged and divided endlessly. There was no easy way to understand them, let alone control them.

But there were always those willing to try. The great landowners – principally the Wittelsbachs, Luxemburgs and Habsburgs – employed every possible tactic to increase their power, from peaceful trade and intermarriage to rob-bery with violence, murder and full-scale war. No estates and no borders were fixtures, especially on the fringes, where the French, the Swiss and the Italians were at it as well. The Habsburgs ruled much of present-day Austria, but they also bought and fought and inherited and married their way into estates that speckled Central Europe from Istria on the Adriatic to northern Holland.

Two rulers attempted to impose peace and unity – the Pope and the German king. Supposedly, their domains were separate, the one looking after the next world across all Europe, the other marshalling Germany's political patch-work. In fact there was no separation. Papal interests were political; royal interests demanded involvement in the Church. To make sense of the confusions would take 600 years of wars and the emergence of another god, Mammon, with his own temples in Brussels.

Christian unity, such as had existed at the fall of the Roman Empire, was virtually a lost cause, because the city of Constantine, whose conversion had made Rome Christian, was now Rome's rival. Both Rome and Constantinople, capitals of the western and eastern rumps of the Empire, regarded themselves as the only true conduit for Christian truth. In Greece and Turkey and much of Eastern Europe, Constantinople (or Byzantium, as it was in Greek) ruled. But Italy and Northern Europe were Rome's. Latinised Christianity had preserved European civilisation for 1,000 years since the collapse of the Roman Empire. Its hundreds of foundations ran schools, built cathedrals – nothing has ever quite equalled that astonishing outpouring of faith, commitment, teamwork and artistry that produced North-ern Europe's Gothic cathedrals – administered estates, dealt with kings and princes. In 1400 modern concepts of scien-tific and historical truth hardly existed – sources were as rare as desert flowers, to be found, if at all, only by a lifetime of travel. The only *true* truth was that of the Church, which, like Big Brother, controlled the media, in the form of scribes (for the written word), priests (for oral transmission) and artists, who served both. The Church had become rich beyond imagining, with the faults that wealth and privilege bring.

Worldly wealth bred corruption at the centre and unrest in subjects appalled by that corruption. In 1300 the Pope, who was French, became so nervous of Italy and its violent ways that he transferred his court to Avignon, where it stayed under French protection for seventy-six years. After a later (Italian) Pope returned to Rome and died, pro-French and pro-Italian factions locked horns on the question of his successor. A botched election produced two rivals, Pope and anti-Pope, one in Avignon, the other in Rome. Both were urged to resign so that a new one could be elected. They both refused, but the compromise candidate was elected anyway. Between 1409 and 1417, the years when Johann Gutenberg was a teenager, there were no fewer than three Popes simultaneously. This long-running farce, known as the Great Schism, for ever damaged papal claims to spiritual and political superiority, and strengthened the case for independence of thought and action among his varied and resentful subjects.

Despite it all, Catholic spiritual authority remained the only unifying force north of the Alps. When Charlemagne had had himself crowned in Rome in 800, he set up a lasting ideal of political and spiritual unity. That idea migrated eastwards with the remains of the Empire itself, emerging under German auspices in the thirteenth century as the Holy Roman Empire (which a later leader would term the First Reich, so he could lay claim to the third one). No German king felt himself to be a proper ruler until crowned emperor by the Pope.

But a papal blessing in Rome buttered few parsnips in the Empire's 400 mini-states. To wield influence, the emperor needed money and soldiers, preferably from imperial estates rather than his own personal possessions. If he was good at the game, he could hope to increase his portfolio with the gain of a church, or a castle, or a river toll, or the income from a Jewish community, or even a whole town. But he could achieve nothing much without the backing of the most powerful of his equals and rivals. In 1356 the German king and leading princes defined the process in a contract known as the Golden Bull. This gave the seven most influential leaders – a king, three archbishops and three nobles – the job of electing the king. From then on, it was as electors that the Big Three – Luxemburgs, Wittelsbachs and Habsburgs – pushed their own candidates for the imperial throne (so called, although technically it was not truly imperial until the papal laying on of hands). No one, of course, wished to give away too much power. So the king/emperor's position remained tenuous. He was always short of money and had no capital from which to administer. His true power-base was local: imperial possessions were few, and anyway kept shifting beneath his feet with every intermarriage, alliance and skirmish. In this federation of wary aristocrats, it was hard for a cash-strapped, peripatetic king to assert himself.

In 1415 an ability to assert himself was what King Sigismund needed above all. Elected in 1411, he was forty-seven and had already lived an eventful and precarious life, typical of the random and obscure nature of events in medieval Germany. As an emperor's son, he was born to the purple, and had connections enough to achieve it. Husband to the queen of Poland, half-brother to the king of Germany, who was also king of Bohemia and brother-in-law to the queen of Poland – his wife's sister, as it happened – he had high hopes of having himself made emperor and restoring the glory that had been Charlemagne's. As a good Christian, he had tried crusading against the Turks and had been lucky to escape with his life. Trying to get his hands on Bohemia, he had arrested his half-brother, been arrested in return, warred against Naples, and had been voted in as German king only because his main rival had died after three months on the throne. So there he was, eager to find a measure of stability in his battered middle age, and to do his best for Christendom, and thus qualify for a papal coronation. Thanks to him, 29 cardinals, 33 archbishops, 150 bishops and their 70,000 courtiers, servants and assistants were at this moment in council in Constance, arguing about how best to overcome the scandal of the Great Schism. Naturally, Sigismund was keen to explore any further way to buttress his authority, and so turned his gaze on unruly Mainz.

❖❖ ❖❖ ❖❖

Mainz, dominating the river-road of the Rhine, lay at the heart of the electoral system. The archbishop of Mainz was an elector, ruling the greatest of the Empire's ten Church-run provinces. It was he who administered the royal coronation oath, which made him a German equivalent of the archbishop of Canterbury. But his status was peculiar to German lands. He was both archbishop, with thirteen bishops under him, and a prince with the power to raise both taxes and armies at will – in theory. In practice, it wasn't that easy, because he had a disputatious flock of patricians and guildsmen, each wanting their say in running the town. It was this dispute that gave Sigismund an excuse to intervene, with an agenda that suited his own purposes both as king and as a Luxemburger. The current archbishop/prince, Johannes of Nassau, had voted against him in the election for king the previous year. He needed to sideline the archbishop by backing the town's council.

Talks focused on hard cash. The archbishop controlled the mint, on Mainz's square across from the cathedral. The council wanted the town to have the right to strike coins. In 1419 Sigismund agreed, hoping that Mainz's new imperial currency would underpin his influence across the whole Rhineland. It didn't work out like that, because the arch-bishop had no intention of allowing an imperial mint to undercut his profits, but for a time it seemed that Mainz would join Frankfurt as a source of new *Apfelgulden* ('apple goldens'), as they were known, after the imperial orb or apple, the *Reichsapfel*, that formed their design.

Through these developments, young Johann Gutenberg would have been busy at his schoolwork, probably at one of the five universities founded in German-speaking lands since the mid-fourteenth century. Possibly he went to Erfurt (founded in 1379), which was popular with students from Mainz, among them two of Johann's cousins. A certain 'Johannes de Altavilla' (the old Latinised name for Eltville) was registered there in 1418 and graduated two years later. If this was our Johann, he was well placed to feel the pulse of the times.

Clerics talked of the ending of the Great Schism at the Council of Constance, of King Sigismund's role as chair-man, and of the continuing unrest in Bohemia. It had started a decade previously with a revolt by the followers of Jan Hus, centring on one of those arcane matters that now seems totally eccentric to outsiders, but which has always been central to Catholicism, indeed all Christianity. It con-cerned the central element in the Eucharist, the Communion service, in which Christians honour Christ's injunction at

the Last Supper to drink wine and eat bread 'in remem-
brance of me'. According to the Roman tradition, bread
alone could be used for the service, if, for instance, no wine
was available (quite a practical policy for missionaries in, say,
Iceland). Not so, claimed the heretical Hus. You had to use
both. Communion had to be dispensed *sub utraque specie*, 'in
both kinds', which gave rise to an alternative name for Hus's
followers, the Utraquists. When one of the Popes called on
Sigismund, the German king, for help, he seized on the
request as an excuse to extend his influence. He offered help,
as long as the Pope agreed to another congress, this time in
the German city of Constance, where he staged a very
public statement of his ambitions. He entered the city on
Christmas Eve 1414, late in the evening, and led his entour-
age into the cathedral, along with locals surging in for the
midnight Mass. Packing the front rows with his followers,
he had himself robed as a priest so that he himself could take
the service. This piece of drama had just the effect he
wanted: the scene formed part of the narrative in a much-
copied picture-history of the council. Here for all the world
to see was the German king in a spiritual role chanting a
Roman liturgy.

Under Sigismund's chairmanship, the council had Hus
burned to death, the Hussites excommunicated *en masse*,
a new Pope (Martin V) elected and further councils
planned. But these were no solutions, for Pope Martin and

council remained at loggerheads and the outraged Hussites declared war, in effect a national uprising. The German burgomaster in Prague was tossed out of the town hall window to the delight of the cheering crowd (incidentally, this seemed to establish a bizarre Czech habit for throwing important people out of windows. A defenestration started the Thirty Years War in 1618 and another marked the coming of Communist rule in 1948.)

All of this would have been common knowledge in Erfurt. Here were professors who had been expelled from Prague when the Hussites decided to promote locals at the expense of the Germans. Gutenberg – assuming he was indeed there – would have spoken with those who predicted dire things for the Hussites, whose obduracy was to obsess both Sigismund and the Pope. He would have listened to the complaints of Czechs and Germans who railed against the corruption of a Church that sold absolutions for cash. He would have been familiar with the names of those in favour of ordinary people reading the Bible, whether in their own language, as John Wycliffe in England proclaimed, or in Latin, or even in Czech (under Hus's influence). From pamphlets printed from woodcuts, he would have learned something of the apparently endless fight between France and England, which we now call the Hundred Years War. He would have acquired a few books, probably buying his own edition – copied at some expense by local scribes – of the most common Latin grammar, the *Ars Grammatica*, by a fourth-century scholar, Aelius Donatus.

By 1420 Johann was back in Mainz, where Archbishop Johannes of Nassau had just died, having lived long enough to see the completion of his ambitious, two-storey cloisters. His statue, brilliantly carved by Mainz's resident genius, Madern Gerthener, was already in place in the cathedral (you can still see it today: third pillar on the right from the altar). Cloisters and statue told the same old story of a Church growing fatter while the town didn't. Johann had little cause for optimism. He had no property of his own, no inherited fortune, and his annuities were at risk. His elder brother, Friele, was in the Gutenberg house with his family. His mother, Else, had moved into a smaller place, though keeping her home in Eltville. His mother's shopkeeping status excluded him from the ranks of the patricians – and thus from the business that would otherwise have provided him with the livelihood he needed.

The business was coin-making. As a Companion of the Mint, his father had been close to it. His uncle, another Johann, was also a Companion. He knew the sons of at least two other Companions, Heinz Reyse and Johann Kumoff, both of whom had shared the Gutenberg house when he was younger. He would have known how coins were struck, because he would have seen the work being done at the mint, on the market square just two minutes' walk from his house.

'Struck' is the operative word here, though technically it is not the coin itself that is struck. Coins were cast from a metal mould; the mould was made from a die, or two dies, with indented surfaces; a die was made with a punch; it was the punch, with its raised pattern, that had to be struck. Anyone, then or now, who has had any experience of jewellery-making or bookbinding would recognise a punch for making coins – a handle like that of a chisel, a steel shank a few centimetres long, on the end of which the punch-maker engraved an image. This shank of engraved steel, correctly positioned on softer metal, was struck with a hammer, leaving a mirror image of itself, as a cattle brand or rubber stamp does. When impressions of two dies (representing both sides of the coin) were ready, they were put together to form the complete mould, into which silver or gold was poured to make the coin.

The key to the operation was the punch. Punch-making in the early fifteenth century was already an ancient art, for which an apprentice punch-maker first learned how to temper steel, heating it and cooling it until it reached a strength that stopped short of brittleness. Then he would learn how to select one of a score of different graving tools, with their minute scooped and angled tips, and scrape away

Striking medals – the fundamental technique for making type. An
eighteenth-century view of a practice little changed from Gutenberg's time
(Woodcut from *Der Weisskunig*, Vienna, 1775. In private ownership)

tiny flakes of steel on the punch's head. It sounds incredible
that steel can cut steel in this way, but if the flakes are small
enough, they peel off easily, until, like a microscopic sculp-

ture, the letter, or figure, or number stood proud from its foundation. The accuracy of a good punch-maker was staggering, and the joy to be taken in it as real as that of any sculptor. Listen to one of our modern punch-makers, Fred Smeijers, a Dutch graphic and typographic designer, waxing lyrical about his skill and his materials in his book *Counterpunch*:

> In order to work correctly and pleasantly your graver has to be sharp. To test its sharpness, just put the graver on your thumbnail. Without any pressure you feel it sinking a little into your naturally very sensitive thumbnail. If you can easily cut curls from the nail of your thumb, then the graver is sharp enough. If we put this graver against the punch at a certain angle, the cutting edge will dig itself into the unhardened steel of the punch. This happens as easily as it did in your thumbnail. With a very light pressure – one can't call it an effort – you push the graver upwards, and by doing this you cut away a little curl of steel. If you keep your hand steady, you can cut away long curls too, even to a length of three millimetres. At moments like this, steel is no longer steel. It looks and feels much more like cold butter: there is the same ease, pressure and pleasure with which you cut off larger and smaller curls of butter with a knife. Then you feel nothing but delight in this

substance, with such a strong and fine structure, which we call steel.

This is truly artistry in miniature, a Western version of those Chinese geniuses who wrote on grains of rice. A curl of steel cut in this way is no more than 0.01 millimetres thick, which is the width of a dot on a dot-matrix printer with a resolution of 6.25 million dots per square inch. By comparison, an early dot-matrix had 90,000–120,000 dpi (dots per square inch). Today's laser printers have a resolution of 750,000 dpi (measured in grains of toner rather than old-fashioned dots, but the terminology endures). Now remember that these minute slivers of steel were no more than 0.01 millimetres thick; they could be as little as a tenth of that, just one micron thick (a thousandth of a millimetre, or a twenty-five-thousandth of an inch).

The startling conclusion is that Johann Gutenberg, from his childhood, was in the company of men who could carve a letter in steel that had at least six, and perhaps sixty, times the resolution of a modern laser printer, just at the time that Sigismund gave Mainz the right to make imperial coins, with a consequent demand for new designs, and new punches.

Did he really do this work himself? I have no idea, and nor does anyone else. There is no evidence one way or the other for all this decade. All we can say with confidence is that he would have known those who did, at a time when that expertise suddenly looked likely to be in demand.

⁘   ⁘   ⁘

And Mainz staggered towards bankruptcy, in a series of financial crises that would take another twenty-six years to run their course. A similar pattern repeated itself every few years: the council, dominated by guildsmen, trying to increase taxes, patricians heading for the countryside, annuities cut, debt repayments reduced, creditors fobbed off, the archbishop bailing out the city, while taking care to keep his ancient privileges intact. In 1430 the archbishop brokered a peace, with complicated clauses about the number of sub-mayors and treasurers, and who should hold copies of keys to the city vaults. Mainz even advertised for immigrants, promising them ten tax-free years. None of it did any good. By 1438 the city would owe 373,000 gulden, enough to buy every house in town. The tensions were intolerable and would eventually, at the end of Gutenberg's life, lead to war.

Johann's elder brother, Friele, came into line, returning with his family to pay taxes and in due course join the new establishment as one of the town's three sub-mayors. But Johann himself seems to have been one of those unwilling to accept the new social order, unable perhaps to see how he could make himself a living. One of his annuities had been cut in half, reducing his income from twenty-three gulden to ten, enough to keep body and soul together for only a few months of the year. He had the good sense, though, to wring from the town clerk, a certain Niklaus von Wörrstadt, a promise by the burgomasters to pay the annuity no matter what; indeed, the harassed clerk even gave him a personal guarantee in case of a default.

Imagine a young man living with the insecurities and fears engendered by random visitations of the Black Death, intensified by social collapse and the threat of civil strife, and deprived of a patrician lifestyle which might so easily have been his. He was in his late twenties, unmarried, intelligent, well educated and (as his later career showed) ambitious. Yet for ten years, even if he was earning pin money as a punch-cutter or coin-maker, he had done nothing of much interest. The only records of him note tedious little changes in his annuities. As he approached thirty, he might well have been feeling a certain frustration.

In 1429 or thereabouts he seems to have made a decision, perhaps inspired by the breakdown of talks between guilds-men and patricians. A conciliation agreement brokered by the archbishop refers to him as 'not in residence' and offered him a chance to return. He refused, and vanished from Mainz's records for the next twenty years. It looks as if he gave up the place as a bad job. For whatever reason, he set out to seek his fortune in a more stable and congenial city.

CHAPTER 2

The Strasbourg Adventure

By 1434 Gutenberg was in Strasbourg, two days upriver from Mainz and a lot more appealing. Strasbourg had been through turmoil similar to Mainz's, but its archbishop was not an elector and its guildsmen had won power more easily. It was now a charming, stimulating and well-off little city-state, with the River Ill running right through it and around its central island, allowing its 25,000 inhabitants easy access to the Rhine, into which the Ill flowed a few kilometres to the east. Its cathedral, a Gothic masterpiece under construction for the previous 150 years, had just acquired the rose window that is still one of the glories of Western art, and the first of its two towers was about to reach its high point, dissolving into a mist of tracery 142 metres up. Stone-built merchants' houses crowded narrow lanes and lined the river, where two cranes served shallow-draught barges. It must have seemed to Gutenberg a delightful base to start on whatever mysterious business he had in mind.

Strasbourg was the seedbed for his life's work. The events of the next ten years probably did not do much to mould his character – he was, after all, in his mid-thirties – but they honed his skills, confirmed his ambitions and revealed traits not seen in him before. They are the traits of a man under stress, not the destructive, out-of-control kind, but the self-chosen, creative stress of an artist, an entrepreneur, even a mountaineer. I think he loved it. He emerges as that rarity: a man seized by an idea, obsessed by it, *imprinted* by it, who also has the technical skill, business acumen and sheer dogged, year-after-year grit to make it real.

⁜   ⁜   ⁜

Gutenberg probably settled on Strasbourg because of family links. His brother Friele had an annuity of twenty-six Strasbourg dinars (a dinar being the local equivalent of a gulden) and would have been a regular visitor there to collect his payments. The clinching event occurred in the summer of 1433, when his mother died, leaving her two houses. The three children agreed a division of the inheritance – Else would have the Gutenberg house in Mainz, Friele would take the one in Eltville, buying out Johann by transferring to him the Strasbourg annuity and his share of the Mainz annuity. With this income, Johann could, in theory, keep clear of Mainz and work in Strasbourg. In practice, things were not so simple, because as far as Mainz's accounts department was concerned, he was out of sight and out of mind, and if he wasn't going to appear in person, Mainz would save its money for more pressing needs.

Gutenberg already had plans, for which he needed all the money he could lay his hands on. We know this from the copy of a document he dictated on 14 March 1434, in which he summarises an incident that must have had all Strasbourg buzzing. One of Mainz's three burgomasters, Niklaus von Wörrstadt − as his home village twelve kilometres south-west of Mainz is now spelled − happened to be in Strasbourg. Niklaus was a tough nut: he had led the guildsmen when they broke off talks with the patricians five years before, and it was he who now had the day-to-day burdens of administering a town continually on the brink of bankruptcy, brought on largely by people whom Gutenberg counted as friends or allies. Like an accountant in many a collapsing company today, he managed by paying only those who applied influence or pressure, a group that for the previous few years had not included Gutenberg. Niklaus was perhaps in town to discuss anti-patrician strategy with his guild colleagues. He had no reason to be looking over his shoulder, no reason even to suspect that one of his aggrieved clients was nearby. Gutenberg, now with friends in places high and low, got wind of Niklaus's presence, saw his chance and pulled out that document hastily signed by the harassed burgomasters of Mainz before his departure, promising that they would *personally* be responsible for the annuity payments.

How the missing sum was calculated is unclear – prob/ably some combination of his own annuities and others inherited from his mother and acquired by arrangement with Friele – but it amounted to 310 gulden. This was enough to buy a substantial house, or pay a staff of ten for a year. Property and labour were cheaper in relative terms then, and today's economies are so vast by comparison that it is hard to come up with a modern equivalent. I find it easier to think in old/fashioned terms, when summer went on for ever and a gulden was worth about £100. In today's terms, we are talking of a sum with the emotional impact of five years' salary all at once, in hard cash, and no income tax or VAT.

He had a grievance; he could prove his case; he knew the local constabulary; and he took action. With a couple of local heavies, he confronted the astonished Niklaus with a demand for payment. Imagine the embarrassment: a visiting dignitary, at supper perhaps, or hurrying off to some appointment with city officials, faced with the news that, as a burgomaster, he had become personally liable for a city debt. Yet there it was, in writing, as Gutenberg said in his statement, duly signed by the 'honourable and wise burgomasters'. I get the impression that he was enjoying this. First the mock humility, then the steely conclusion –

by the contract, the *honourable and wise* burgomasters agreed that in the event of default 'I may serve on them a writ of attachment, imprison them and seize their property'. I can almost see Niklaus's appalled expression, the dawning realisation that Gutenberg was serious. Off went Niklaus to the debtors' prison.

Gutenberg's actions suggest a sharp mind and a deter-mined character, seizing the initiative at just the right moment. He knew that Mainz was strapped for cash, that his old acquaintance and adversary, Niklaus, had the power to cough up on the city's behalf. This was not personal, though. Niklaus was merely the lever to get the money. Any hint of a personal vendetta would not have gone down well with Strasbourg officials, who would have to repair the damage done to inter-town relations. And the remedy was easy. All Niklaus had to do was to promise to pay, within a reasonable time, say two months, which as a current burgomaster he could do. Everyone knew this. No doubt Gutenberg was able to reassure them not to worry, there would be no lasting damage, and with 310 gulden on the way there could well be a little something for those willing to see this matter to its rightful conclusion. With everyone looking to him to ensure a happy outcome, he could afford to be magnanimous.

So it turned out. Niklaus made his promise and regained his freedom. Gutenberg smoothed his ruffled feathers, promising, out of the goodness of his heart, that he would not hold Niklaus personally liable for any future arrears. And Niklaus was as good as his word, arranging for the town to pay up, through Gutenberg's cousin, Ort Gelthus, who lived in Oppenheim, ten kilometres upriver from Mainz. In Strasbourg, Gutenberg would have acquired a certain reputation among those who counted: hard-nosed, decisive, but fair-minded. A man to watch.

By the agreed date – Pentecost, seven weeks after Easter – Gutenberg had enough money to start work. He rented a place in a hamlet hard by a monastery named after a local fifth-century bishop, St Arbogast, a couple of kilometres or so up the River Ill, where the river broke into charming backwaters, running around a couple of islands and flowing out over a flood plain opposite. Here he employed Lorenz Beildeck and his wife as servants. What he was up to was anyone's guess, but it was something that needed privacy. In town, eyes pried, tongues wagged and city ordinances forbade the use of forges for fear of fire. Out in the country, he was free to experiment, while building a network of contacts in town that would stand him in good stead later. He seems to have cultivated people of all classes, from craftsmen to patricians and aristocrats. In these hierarchical times, it seems he was disconcertingly hard to pigeonhole. In the few surviving documents he is referred to variously as a goldsmith, a non-guildsman and a member of Strasbourg's upper classes.

Here, then, we have a well-off man, with staff and good contacts and a substantial household which included a remarkably well-stocked wine cellar – he paid tax on something over 1.5 *Fuder* of wine in July 1439. A *Fuder* is a barrel containing 1,000 litres. Given that oxidation would reduce wine to vinegar within a year, this is a generous amount. It suggests that he had laid in a store, at his own expense, of wine enough for a household of ten or a dozen people, each of whom could get through half a litre every day (though it was usual then for wine to be diluted, which would have extended its consumption time).

☙ ☙ ☙

He was in his mid-thirties, established, engaged on some important work or other, well off and unmarried. And so, as is the way of things, there was a girl. Her name was Ennelin. The evidence is slight – copies of two court-case summaries made in 1436–7 – and it has been the cause of much academic wrangling about whether Ennelin existed and whether Gutenberg married her or not. But it is now possible to make sense of what happened, with a few tantalising gaps.

Ennelin was real enough. She came from a patrician family named after a property known as 'the Iron Door'. Ennelin (a version of Änna-lein) is a diminutive of Anna. Ennelin zur

Yserin Thüre (zur Eisernen Tür, in modern German) could be rendered in English as Little Annie Iron Door. I like to imagine that she was drawn to this self-contained, enigmatic inventor working out in the country a mere twenty-minute walk from town. If there was an affair, it was more likely one of the heart alone, probably her heart more than his, since her family was high class and Gutenberg had a certain standing. To be sure, he was no casual womaniser.

It was Ennelin's mother, Ellewibel, who caused the fuss. There's no father in this story, so she was the stern guardian of her daughter's virtue and interests. At first, it seems, she approved of the relationship, for here was a man of good repute, running a large household, with ambitious plans and a reputation for decisive action – he was the one who put that upstart guildsman from Mainz in his place. He would have been quite a catch.

But Gutenberg never had any intention of marrying Ennelin. He was far too involved with his work. When Ellewibel wanted to name the day, having no doubt talked to friends, neighbours and relatives, it was a shock to discover that there would be no marriage day. Mrs Iron Door became a very angry patrician, outraged on her daughter's behalf, and horribly embarrassed. She wanted revenge. The only thing open to her was to sue Gutenberg for breach of promise. She scouted round for witnesses and found one in Claus Schott, a local shoemaker. As the record of the case shows, she laid her complaint, backed up by Schott.

Gutenberg was completely flabbergasted. He had never promised anything! Who was this Schott character anyway, he asked the gentlemen of the Church court where the case was heard, and then, in a fury, answered his own question: 'A miserable wretch who lives by cheating and lying!' Schott was outraged in his turn and demanded legal redress: hence the second surviving court record. The court agreed that he had been publicly insulted, and ordered Gutenberg to pay fifteen gulden for defamation.

And there the evidence runs out. We have no idea whether Ellewibel proved her case and got anything for her trouble. Probably not. Anyway, there was no marriage. Mother and daughter were still living together seven years later, according to city records, and then we hear nothing more of them. How did the lovers (if they were lovers) meet? Was Ennelin a heady teenager eager to evade her mother's eagle eye? Or did Ellewibel engineer the relation-ship in the hope of making a good match for a dull daughter? Did Ennelin recover, and marry, or nurse a broken heart into a nunnery? It's unlikely we will ever know.

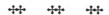

What was Gutenberg doing while out at St Arbogast? One thing is certain: he wanted to make money, a lot of it.

Perhaps that was the extent of his ambitions at this moment. Or perhaps the idea of printing was already in his mind, and he was busy working on problems and solutions. If so, he would have discovered that he needed far more capital than he had available. To get it, he needed some additional scheme that would make money immediately, so that he could put it to long-term use. Either way, he had an idea.

To understand the idea and its brilliance, we have to take a small detour to the wilder shores of religious eccentricity. The journey takes us 250 kilometres northwards, to the city of Aachen. This was the revered capital of Charlemagne – Karolus Magnus, or Charles the Great – founder of the Empire, the fount of both its holiness and its Roman-ness. In the cathedral, the greatest of its age, Charlemagne was buried. Here in 1000, the German king Otto III, who dreamed of reuniting Christendom, sought to imbue himself with Charlemagne's magic by opening the tomb of his hero beneath the glorious octagonal choir. Tradition claims that he found the great king crowned and sceptred, seated on a throne 'as though he lived', uncorrupted except for a little decay in the nose. The corpse was wearing gloves through which the nails had grown. Otto re-dressed the body in white, cut the nails, gave it a new nose of gold and 'made all good', or so they said. Perhaps something of this was true, for Otto placed Charlemagne's white-marble throne on the first-floor gallery, where it stood as the centrepiece for the coronations of German kings for another 500 years, and still stands today. After Otto's day, the shrine, like all great shrines, attracted a collection of holy relics, the authenticity of which no one in these credulous times dreamed of questioning. In 1165 Charlemagne became a saint, and his remains, placed in a golden casket, were revered along with the relics.

The collection became a focus of one of the greatest of medieval pilgrimages. Demand grew until in the mid-fourteenth century the authorities formalised access by displaying the relics every seven years. Thereafter, in pilgrimage years many thousands streamed into the cathedral to gaze in awe at the swaddling clothes of the Christ-child, the loincloth of the crucified Christ, the Virgin's robe and the cloth that held John the Baptist's severed head. In the early fifteenth century the pressure of pilgrims became more than the cathedral could take. Aachen again bowed to popular demand and made arrangements for the relics to be shown outside, on a wooden stage, on which dignitaries held up the items one by one. Now the crowds could come in even greater numbers. In the 1432 pilgrimage, 10,000 people a day thronged the cathedral close, in a mood verging on hysteria. During the next pilgrimage, the crush was so great that a building collapsed, killing seventeen and injuring a hundred. This was the culmination of weeks on the road. All hoped for . . . they knew not what exactly, but all were tense in expectation of some life-changing experience. As proof of their visit, they bought little metal badges, seven to ten centimetres high, decorated with a saint or two, a Virgin and child, or two priests holding up Mary's robe.

The holy relics were, of course, considered to be powerful charms. They could soothe hearts and souls and bodies, because, so it was believed, healing streams issued from them like invisible solar rays. Once, pilgrims could hope to touch the relics and thus partake of their powers. Now that was impossible, what with the crush of people and the relics so far off. What a terrible waste it was – all that healing power flowing away unused into space, when back home were the destitute and diseased longing for the touch of someone who had actually touched the relics of Aachen. By the early fifteenth century the idea got around that technology could provide a solution. People were beginning to use spectacles for reading. Lenses were not yet of glass; clear crystals were used, particularly beryl. (Germans called these devices 'Berylle', which eventually contracted to 'Brille', the modern word for spectacles.) But glass *mirrors* were popular – Nuremberg had a guild of mirror-makers by the late fourteenth century – and there was a good market among the well-off for little convex mirrors that seemed to capture the wide world. You can see one on the wall in Jan van Eyck's portrait of the Bruges merchant Giovanni Arnolfini, done in 1434.

Now we get to the nub of the matter, for in Aachen, in the 1432 pilgrimage, word spread that a convex mirror, by capturing a wide-angle view, would absorb the healing radiance of the holy relics. Suddenly, everyone wanted a badge with a mirror, just a simple round twelve-millimetre mirror, not of glass but of polished metal, set in its lead or copper frame, with its crude emblematic figures. (Mirrors made of glass – 'ox-eyes' as they were known – came later, and remained a fad through the sixteenth century.) Once you had your mirror, you found some suitable vantage point – even the city walls were crowded – where you could hold the mirror aloft, the longer the better, as if it were a third eye, allowing it to be imbued with the rays of holiness. Now your tourist trinket had turned into a thing of power, full of radiant energy. You could head for home in the secure and happy knowledge that you carried in your belt-pouch the very essence of the miraculous. If you arrived before the effect faded, why, you could be the one to straighten limbs and cure the plague. The mirror was as much a guarantee of satisfaction as a photograph of the Pope or a rock hero's T-shirt.

The problem in 1432 was that the goldsmiths and stamp-makers of Aachen could not possibly meet the demand. What a demand it was, what a market, what a point of sale: 10,000 people every day for two weeks. The local guildsmen agreed that, for the brief time of the pilgrimage, outsiders

could make and sell pilgrim badges and mirrors. It was a
licence to print money, or rather strike coins (as the records
show: at a later pilgrimage, in 1466, 130,000 badges were
sold).

This was Gutenberg's inspiration: he would mass-
produce mirrors for the 1439 Aachen pilgrimage.

His plan was to make 32,000 mirrors, selling at half a
gulden each. A little piece of metal for £50 or so? It sounds
high. But that was what the locals charged, that was what
the pilgrims were prepared to pay. So the bottom line was a
return of 16,000 gulden on an expenditure of 600 gulden –
a profit of 2,500 per cent. It was like investing £100,000
and getting back £2.5 *million*. Either Gutenberg had his
sums wrong – not likely, given his experience – or he was on
his way to a fortune. There were just two little problems: no
one had mass-produced mirrors in this way, and he didn't
have 600 gulden to spare.

What, you may ask, has all this to do with printing? Two
things. One was the money needed to develop an entirely new
technology; the other was the possible relationship between
the techniques of making mirrors and the techniques of
printing books. Both needed presses, though what role they
filled in badge-making or mirror-making is unclear. The
evidence that Gutenberg was working on a press of some
kind is clear enough; that he was working on a *printing* press
at this stage is pure conjecture. Historians have been inclined

to argue that the work of the mirrors was a stepping-stone, whether conscious or not, towards the work of the books. In fact, as the events unfold, it will make sense to see the two operations as entangled with each other, but in ways that will probably remain for ever hidden.

✣✣ ✣✣ ✣✣

In 1438 Gutenberg acquired three partners. Hans Riffe, Andreas Dritzehn and Andreas Heilmann were local worthies. There were no *von*s and *zu*s in their names, no big properties behind them, but their forebears had worked their way up from crafts and trades to eminence in business and local government. Riffe, for instance, was a prefect of the outlying suburb of Lichtenau and had brothers who were provosts in the St Arbogast monastery, near which Gutenberg was living. They were men of sound standing and, one would have thought, sound judgement. Yet, like many other investors since, they became enamoured of an idea, and lost their money.

We know they lost, because the venture came apart in circumstances beyond their control. Ahead there lay worries, a death, a dispute, a court case. It is from the witnesses called in that case and the final judgement that we know anything of all this — not enough to explain the really significant part, because the surviving partners were still possibly within reach of a fortune that depended, crucially, on secrecy. So the evidence is frustrating. Whenever witnesses get near the point, they clam up. Mirrors they could mention. A press they could mention. But there was something else in hand which they could not. No one even introduced into court the contract that bound them, presumably for fear that it would reveal their secret. Like alchemists who knew they had within reach the philosopher's stone that would turn all to gold, they clapped hands over mouths and muttered only of the 'common work', the 'art', the 'adventure'.

The words 'adventure and art' – *aventur und kunst* – have become a key to a treasure for researchers. The treasure, of course, is the invention of printing with movable type. We know it was in the air, because we have the results, the printed books, which came several years later. But was this the same treasure that the partners were so anxious to guard? The answer to this question is the Holy Grail of Gutenberg research, and much paper has passed through many presses in the pursuit of an answer. No one has yet found it, though the circumstantial evidence suggests scenarios galore.

The surviving evidence for this chapter in Gutenberg's life has its own story. Actually, there isn't any genuine surviving evidence, at least not *original* evidence. The depositions were part of two volumes of court records, written by the same scribe on sheets a little smaller than today's standard typing paper, as some of us still quaintly call it. From the day they were written and filed away in 1439, they lay in Strasbourg's archives, little changed by the passage of time, for almost 300 years, until they were noticed by local researchers, copied and published in 1760. Then the originals were destroyed. One volume joined fifteen wagonloads of records burned on 12 November 1793 by French soldiers after the city fell to Napoleon's armies. The second volume went up in flames with the city library in 1870. What survives is a copy, which is itself incomplete, perhaps because some of the original pages were missing. But there is no reason to doubt that what we have – thirteen of twenty-five witness statements, and the final judgement – is true to the original.

So to the evidence. It is as confusing as the stuff of countless other trials. Witnesses are contradictory, forgetful, biased and thoroughly, vividly, infuriatingly human. There is no coherent narrative in the extracts. To make them tell a story is like trying to reconstitute a movie from a couple of dozen rough-cuts.

Here are the scenes, in an order that makes the most sense of the conflicting evidence. The body-copy is paraphrased; the quotes are as authentic as I can make them in translation:

1.   Andreas Dritzehn begs to join Gutenberg in developing his business. Gutenberg teaches him to 'polish stone' or 'stones'.

2.   Between 1435 and 1438 a goldsmith, Hans Dünne, earns 100 gulden 'just for that which pertains to the pressing'. (Incidentally, the phrase Dünne uses is '*zu dem trucken*' – '*zum Drucken*', as it would be today, which in modern German means 'to the printing'. Modern German makes a distinction between '*drucken*', 'to print', and '*drücken*', 'to press', but before printing made its mark in around 1500 there was no such umlauted linguistic difference. At the time, it could have meant either. My feeling is that if printing was already under way in 1438, Dünne would have been a little more careful with his language.)

3.   In early 1438 Gutenberg and Hans Riffe agree that Riffe will help finance the production of mirrors for the Aachen pilgrimage, profits to be divided 2:1.

4.   Andreas Dritzehn begs to be included in the partnership and offers his labour. Andreas Heilmann also talks his way in. All four come to an agreement to split the profits as follows: Gutenberg: 50 per cent; Riffe: 25 per cent; Dritzehn: 12.5 per cent; Heilmann: 12.5 per cent.

5.   On 22 or 23 March – two or three days before the Annunciation (25 March) – the two Andreases

pay the first eighty gulden each for instruction in 'the new art, which he would teach them'. But Andreas Dritzehn is already overstretched, because he has to borrow some of the money from two friends.

Bottom line to date (rounded): 1,000 gulden, of which 500 is in cash.

6.   Outwardly, all is peace and harmony. Andreas Dritzehn loads a cart with a barrel of brandy, a 500-litre barrel of wine and several baskets of pears and takes them out to St Arbogast for Gutenberg to repay his hospitality. Work continues.

7.   Summer 1438: bad news. The plague returns, spreading north from Italy to Aachen, and the authorities announce that the 1439 pilgrimage is to be delayed by a year – and so, therefore, are profits from the sale of the mirrors.

8.   The two Andreases pay an unannounced visit to Gutenberg and discover he 'knows of another secret art'. They think Gutenberg has been holding out on them, perhaps planning to use their money by making a second, even more profitable enterprise riding on the back of the first. The 'secret art'

increases the appeal of Gutenberg's business. Now they want to get in deeper.

9. Gutenberg insists on formalising matters with a new agreement. The two promise to pay an additional sum, in stages, in effect doubling the size of the enterprise and their own contributions. Riffe either does not come in on the new deal or is sidelined. The agreement is to last five years. It includes a clause stating that in the event of a death, 100 gulden will be repaid to the heirs.

10. Andreas Dritzehn is struggling. He raises some of the cash through a broker, against the security of his assets, but still cannot pay the agreed sum.

11. Dritzehn is a worried man. He is talking to a trades-woman, Bärbel, who is from Zabern (now Saverne, forty kilometres north-west of Strasbourg) and is either staying with him or has come by for a drink. It's late. Dritzehn is doing his accounts.

    She says: 'Aren't we *ever* going to bed?' (Her reported words are: '*Wollen wir heute nicht mehr schlafen?*' Literally: 'Do we not wish today no more to sleep?' Most English versions translate the sentence with a 'you' instead of a 'we', which could work, but puts a distance between the two. I like the implied asperity of a close friend – though not too close, for she calls him by the polite second person *ihr*, the equivalent of French *vous*, while he addresses her with the familiar *du*. On such subtleties does the imagination thrive.)

Dritzehn is not to be deflected. 'I have to finish this first.' Note he says 'I', not 'we'; they're not together in this work.

'God help us!' says Bärbel. 'What's the point of spending all this money? It's probably cost you ten gulden already.'

'You're an idiot if you think it's cost me only ten gulden!'

Imagine her eyebrows raised in a query: how much then?

He wriggles under her gaze, wondering about the secret he is guarding and his business reputation. More than 300 . . . Quite a bit more, actually . . . Enough over 300 to keep you going for the rest of your life . . . Well, all right, almost 500. To be more precise, he probably spent about 350, with another eighty-five still to find. His possessions, his inheritance – all pledged as security. Now he's reached his limit.

'Suffering Jesus!' says Bärbel. 'What if it goes

wrong? What will you do then?'

'Nothing can go wrong. Within a year we'll get our capital back, and we'll all be in bliss.'

'*Uns kann nichts misslingen*' – 'nothing can go wrong'. Andreas Dritzehn has never heard of tempting fate.

12. December 1438: Andreas borrows another eight gulden from a friend, which he secures with a ring worth thirty gulden (the witness, Reimbolt, is not rich: he gets five gulden for it from the Jewish pawnbroker in his home village, Ehenheim). Andreas also borrows more from Reimbolt's housekeeper. But he is still about eighty gulden short of the final agreed sum due to Gutenberg.

13. Gutenberg becomes nervous that his secret will fall into the wrong hands. He sends his servant, Lorenz Beildeck, to the two Andreases 'to fetch all the forms' (a 'form' or 'forme' is the term later used for a page of type, but there is no certainty that it meant that to Gutenberg, at least not yet). The 'formes' are to be brought and melted down, 'so that no one saw it' (whatever 'it' was). This was done, to Gutenberg's distress at seeing his work return to the melting-pot.

This is revealing, because up until now it has been a fair assumption that Gutenberg is supervising the work in person in St Arbogast. Apparently not – the 'adventure and art' is based at least in part in Strasbourg, otherwise there would be no need to send Beildeck on his errand.

14. Christmas 1438: Andreas Dritzehn falls mortally ill. He is in bed at the house of a friend, the witness Midehard Stocker. Andreas tells the details of the partnership, and says with remarkable prescience: 'I know I'm going to die. If I should die, I'll wish I had never got into this partnership, because I know my brothers will never come to an agreement with Gutenberg.'

15. 26 December: Andreas Dritzehn dies. Panic among the surviving partners that the winding-up of his affairs will draw attention to the press and blow their secret.

16. 27 December: Andreas Heilmann asks the maker of the press, Konrad Sassbach, to 'take the pieces from the press and separate them, so that no one can know what it is'. Again, the enigmatic 'it'. But when they go along, 'there was the thing, gone'.

Gutenberg shares the concern. It seems that melting the 'formes' is not security enough. He, too, is worried about 'four pieces' that the late Andreas left 'lying in a press'. He again sends Beildeck to town, this time to Andreas Dritzehn's brother, Claus. Claus is to take these out of the press and undo 'both screws so that the pieces fell apart' so that if anyone sees them and the press 'they would not be able to see or work out what it was'. (It!) Then, after the funeral, he should go out to see Gutenberg, who had something to talk over with him. Claus Dritzehn goes to look for the pieces, but he, like Heilmann and Sassbach, fails to find anything. Someone else, it seems, has taken or hidden it, or them.

17.   Andreas Dritzehn's other brother, Jörg, wants him and Claus to inherit Andreas's share in the partnership, and in the secret. Gutenberg demurs. Jörg tries to force Gutenberg's hand by suing him. (The late Andreas was right – the two surviving Dritzehns were indeed vexatious characters. During the lawsuit, Lorenz Beildeck formally complained about Jörg's insulting remarks; six years later the two brothers sued each other over Andreas's estate, which included both a 'cutting instrument' and a press.)

18. In December 1439 the court agrees with Gutenberg. He can repay the Dritzehns a small sum, which together with what Andreas had not paid makes up the 100 gulden owed on the death of a partner. The rest of the money stays tied up in the business. Gutenberg is free to pursue whatever project he has in hand. The secret remains secure.

✢✢   ✢✢   ✢✢

Was this project actually printing, as a little memorial stone on a river island named after Gutenberg claims and as several historians have argued since? Or merely a step in that direction?

It would help to know how the mirrors were actually produced, and in what way the techniques could be used for printing. The question has no answer, for we have none of Gutenberg's mirrors (though a few made by others), and no records. But the scale of the operation offers some insight. Gutenberg had a market of 100,000-plus pilgrims to exploit. Of course, he could not saturate the market, but even to supply a tenth of it would demand a tonne of lead and tin, melted together to form an alloy. It was a small industrial operation, with metal to be bought, delivered and processed. Gutenberg seemed well able to handle the work, both as technician and as businessman. Capital flow, terms of partnership, budget and projected return were all wrapped up in a contract, which, as the lawsuit with Jörg showed, was well enough understood and agreed to stand up in court.

To review the evidence: there was a press, probably in Andreas Dritzehn's house. Some sort of smelting work was going on in St Arbogast. There were 'formes' and 'four pieces' held together by 'two screws' in one of the Heilmann houses. The goldsmith, Hans Dünne, could have done engraving work. It sounds very much as if this is the basis for an embryonic or experimental printing operation, with a punch-cutter (Dünne), a typefounder (Gutenberg), type set into 'formes', and a press.

All very interesting, but hardly something to seize minds and drive men half-mad with fears of industrial espionage. The press, apparently central to the operation, would not have been all that remarkable, because presses had been used since ancient times to make wine and extract oil, and more recently to squeeze paper dry. The other materials and items needed for this still-hypothetical printing operation would not have been all that remarkable either – the punches, which were also used for making medals, coins, armour and the metal decorations on furniture; parchment – dried animal skin – which had been used as a writing material since the third century BC; paper, parchment's cheaper substitute, the production of which had spread from Asia via Spain 300 years previously and now involved half a dozen paper-mills in Germany; the ink, which was in common use by textile manufacturers, artists and woodblock printers. Surely, a business with such established elements would not have attracted the attention of local businessmen, or taken so long to develop, or been a process that had to be kept under wraps.

So what am I missing? Well, there are two vital elements I haven't mentioned, which together mark Gutenberg's invention – not mere printing, but printing with movable type – as a work of a genius. One is an intellectual leap, the other its technical application. He was still at the research and development stage – hence the time, money and secrecy – but both ideas were simple enough for anyone to have grasped the principle, seen the potential and run off with them. It was, I believe, the combination of the two elements that were at the secret heart of his 'adventure and art'.

CHAPTER 3

A Hercules Labouring for Unity

𝕋here is a cliché about inventions that they burst to life in the minds of poverty-stricken loners, who struggle in garrets to turn brilliant novelties into material form. Not in Gutenberg's case. He was quite well off, he was a great team worker, and most of the materials and devices for his invention existed before he came along. Yes, there was a heart to printing with movable type that he set beating, but the existence of the body of knowledge suggested to me some sort of inspiration from his world. If so, what form might it have taken?

The search promised to be hard going, taking me into the confused heart of Gutenberg's Europe. This supposed Christian unity was splintered by rivalries and antipathies: Pope *v.* anti-Pope, German emperor *v.* one Pope or other, warlords *v.* emperor, Catholics *v.* Hussites, and Pope *v.* his council of senior prelates, the last being of particular concern at a time when Church leaders were wrangling over the nature of papal authority. And that's just Europe, minus the grandest rivalry of all, Rome *v.* Constantinople, where the Byzantine emperor ruled over a Christian world apart, with its own theological and political disputes. Since it was surely God's will that peace and unity should reign, it was the ardent desire of each well-meaning prelate and prince to bring peace to this seething mass of unrest, provided only that peace could be made on his own terms. Such intransigence ensured enduring conflict.

Fortunately, there was someone who may have played a special role in this story. He was a contemporary of Guten-berg, not a born leader, who willed Christian unity as much as any prince, and brought to the task greater subtlety, strength of character and intellect than most. Several historians have suspected him of being the hidden hand focusing the rays that lit the fuse that led to Gutenberg's explosive invention. The evidence is soft and circumstantial, but even if he wasn't the inventor's muse, his life overlapped with Gutenberg's in intriguing ways and acts as a lens through which to observe his world.

His name was Nicholas (Nikolaus in German), and he came from Kues, sometimes spelled with a C after its Roman name, Cusa. Now linked with Bernkastel, its sister town across the River Mosel, Kues lies just eighty kilometres west of Mainz among Germany's best and prettiest vineyards. Nicholas of Cusa – Cusanus as he was known in Latin – was famous in his life, but then mostly forgotten until a Cusanus renaissance in Germany in the mid-nineteenth century. Immensely learned German philosophers started a waterfall of scholarship which poured down to the present, gathering pace along the way, turning him into a cult figure in some academic circles. When in the 1920s Ernst Cassirer, the heaviest of the heavies, wrote of Cusanus in *Individual and Cosmos in Renaissance Philosophy*, he dedicated the book to the Jewish philanthropist Amy Warburg, scion of the eminent banking family. Amy Warburg was the founder of the Warburg Library in Hamburg; with Hitler's rise to power in 1933, the library moved to London as the Warburg Institute. The Warburg Institute contains a fine collection of Cusaniana, with works about him in English, French, German and Italian. But the British, for some reason, are not Cusanus groupies, and the Warburg's shelves are a puddle compared with the lakes of scholarship elsewhere. Tap 'Cusanus' into an Internet search engine, and you stumble on Cusanus societies in both America and Japan, while the University of Trier, close to his birthplace, has a major research institute entirely devoted to him, based on the library of books and manuscripts he left on his death.

He owes his stature to his astonishing range of interests

and the depth, not to say obscurity, of his philosophy. Here's an example:

> Since the absolutely Maximum is all that which can be, it is altogether actual. And just as there cannot be anything greater, so for the same reason there cannot be anything lesser, since it is all that which can be. But the Minimum is that than which there cannot be a lesser. And since the Maximum is also such, it is evident that the Maximum coincides with the Minimum.

Such thoughts combine with speculations that sometimes smack of startling modernity. He suggested, for instance, that the earth is in motion and that the universe has no centre, which sounds as if he was anticipating Copernicus and Einstein. Was this anathema to the Church, as Copernicus's theories were a century later? Not at all, for his ideas have their roots in a standard medieval concern with God as infinity. His astronomical ideas are derived from voracious reading and deep thought, not from observation or experiment. His thinking was rooted in what he called 'learned ignorance', *docta ignorantia*, based on the notion that the purpose of knowledge is to learn how inadequate all learning is when seeking God. This is why the Japanese love him – they regard him as an honorary Buddhist. His theology, expressed in dense Latin, is a cloud of transcendence which can be used for an infinity of research and argument.

His philosophy was of no direct concern to Gutenberg, but it had practical applications in politics. Nicholas, like his co-theologians, knew God as the Infinite, the All-Embracing, the Ultimate in which Maximum and Minimum were one. If God was, in his words, the *coincidentia oppositorum* – the coincidence of opposites – then his creation, too, ought to be a unity, which it self-evidently wasn't. Its current state of political disunity was an abomination to Nicholas. His whole life was defined by an obsession to make opposites coincide, to establish the unity that was foreshadowed by ancient Rome and Charlemagne, and which ought now to find expression, in the German Empire and/or the papacy and/or all Christendom. The struggle to resolve the tensions between these elements provided the context for his life as a working politician and lawyer. In this respect he was thoroughly down to earth, travelling incessantly, talking, persuading, writing, as if these were the tools with which he would stitch together a fragmented Christian commonwealth.

One of those tools could have been the word of God, in print.

❖❖ ❖❖ ❖❖

Nicholas was born in 1401, which makes him pretty much the same age as Gutenberg, of a father who was no aristocrat, but well off nevertheless, with a boat business and several houses. According to tradition, Nicholas was educated at a school set up in the late fourteenth century by a group of laymen, the Brethren of the Common Life, in Deventer in the Netherlands. The Brethren were mystics who devoted themselves to a simple, communal life and care of the poor, in 'imitation of Christ' (the title of a book by their most famous member, Thomas à Kempis). They also promoted scholarship, by producing books, hand-copied ones and then block-printed ones. The 'Brothers of the Quill', as they were widely known, were proud to spread the Word 'not by word but by script'. Mysticism, scholarship, writing and the idea and significance of repro-ducing information – these were passions that were built into Nicholas in his youth and were to run through his life.

After student days in Heidelberg and Padua, where he studied law, maths and astronomy, he returned as a newly qualified 'canon lawyer' – a specialist in Church law – to the Rhineland, where in 1427 he became secretary to the archbishop of Trier, and then, as word of his legal skills spread, secretary to the papal legate in Germany, Cardinal Giordano Orsini. It was the beginning of his career as an ecclesiastical lawyer and statesman, to support which he began to gather a portfolio of so-called benefices, acquiring the right to administer parishes through a deputy priest – and also administer the income they made. This practice was technically against ecclesiastical law, but since the law could be changed by papal dispensation, 'pluralism', as it was known, became a common scam for those of influence, ambition and no inherited wealth. Canon lawyers were particularly adept pluralists.

The late 1420s was a significant time to start such a career, for both Church and Empire confronted a double crisis:

- the rumbling dispute between a Pope aiming for absolute power and the council of prelates who had recently got rid of anti-Popes, saved the Church from anarchy and thought that their current pro-tégé, Martin V, owed them deference;
- and the rebellion in Bohemia of the Hussites, who had been up in arms since that treacherous burning of their leader in 1415. Bohemia was fast becoming a quagmire, Christian Europe's Vietnam. Two papal invasions of their land ended in two ignom-inious defeats, the last in 1431, when 130,000 imperial troops were scattered by phalanxes of farm carts used as war wagons, and the Pope's repre-sentative, Cardinal Giuliano Cesarini, had to flee for his life in disguise.

At the same time as imperial troops were invading Bohemia, the next council was supposed to be opening in Basel, one of its aims being to resolve the Hussite rebellion. The Pope was to be represented by the same Cardinal Cesarini who was on his way to defeat at the hands of the Hussites. In mid-February 1431, two weeks before the council's planned opening, Pope Martin died. At a time when it took months to gather for pan-European conferences like this, progress became glacial. Leaders drifted in every couple of weeks. By July only a dozen delegates had arrived in time for the opening ceremony in the cathedral. Six weeks later, Cesarini finally appeared after his narrow escape, now representing a new Pope, Eugenius IV. Since the council would last for years — eighteen, as it turned out — and would, perhaps, create enduring peace in Europe, leaders took care to make their mark. Princes with magnificent entourages came from Burgundy, Hungary, France, Germany, Italy and Spain. The Castilians arrived with 1,400 horses and twenty-eight mules, attended by pages clad in silver. The first public session in December passed, and still they came, bishops, abbots, priors and professors all turning Basel from a little backwater into a temporary capital, building up to full strength of almost 400 delegates over the next eighteen months, until King Sigismund himself deemed the time right for his own appearance.

In February 1432 Nicholas, the lawyer from Trier, arrived. His official task was to put the case for a new boss who, on the death of his old one, Trier's archbishop, had laid claim to the archbishopric. But he had more than his client's interests in mind.

✢✢ ✢✢ ✢✢

By that stage it is possible, just possible, that Nicholas and Gutenberg had met. They would have found they had much in common. They were two young men of similar back‑grounds: well‑off families, neither of them noble, both irked by a class structure that limited them. They came from the same area, and Nicholas was in Mainz on several occasions. He was there briefly for a court case in 1424. Perhaps they met then, these two twenty‑four‑year‑olds, both newly qualified, the canon lawyer aiming high and the restless technocrat looking to use his skills to set up in business.

Even if they did meet, it would have taken time for their ideas to come together. So perhaps it was a later meeting — sometime between 1428 and 1432, after Gutenberg left Mainz and before Nicholas arrived in Basel — that planted the germ of an idea, which could have emerged like this: Nicholas wanted Christian unity, a dream he pursued from his postgraduate days onwards; unity would be under‑pinned by every Christian across Europe repeating the same words, reading the same texts, saying the same prayers, literally singing from the same song‑book; for that to happen, Christianity needed uniformity in its texts.

What if Nicholas of Cusa and Johann Gutenberg shared this vision of somehow, no one knew how, duplicating texts to perfection?

The time was just right. Nicholas, off to Basel to fight the case for his candidate for the Trier archbishopric, would be in touch with people with the fate of all Europe in their hands. The key to influence, they would have agreed, was the book.

For 300 years now, the production of books had brought Christians ever further and ever faster out of the age of dark⁄ness that had descended on Europe after the fall of Rome. The flame of learning, tended for a thousand years in a thousand monasteries, burned brighter by the year. Religious books were easier to read, with capital letters marked with colour, and chapter divisions. No longer did monks mutter out loud as they read, as if reading was a form of talk; people actually read to themselves, in silence. As trade links grew and towns evolved, learning escaped from the cloister, and ordinary peo⁄ple began to send their children to school, to learn the three Rs as well as Latin, the language of religion and thus of learning. Universities arose from about 1350, with a consequent demand for books. As paper made from rags became more popular, so books became cheaper. Merchants' offices and city halls had their scribes, and the scribes acquired assistants, and all needed an education, and the teachers needed books, and so literacy spiralled, feeding itself. One Italian entrepreneur,

Francesco di Marco Datini of Prato, left 140,000 letters when he died in 1410. People, particularly Italians living in a score of trade-rich city-states, already knew they were in the midst of an intellectual and artistic fermentation; the Renaissance was one of those few historical periods that discovered itself, rather than being defined by hindsight.

In this process, Nicholas of Cusa, the multicultural Renaissance man from Germany, played a leading part, not only in philosophy. In 1429 he brought to Rome manu-scripts that contained twelve plays by the Latin comedy writer, Plautus, which, when published (thirteen editions by 1500), influenced European comedy from then on. Nicholas Udall, who wrote the first English comedy, *Ralph Roister Doister* (1552), owes a debt of thanks to Plautus's *Miles Gloriosus*, and its rediscoverer, Nicholas. So do Shakespeare (*The Taming of the Shrew*), Molière (*The Miser*) and many others, even the modern French playwright Jean Giraudoux, whose *Amphitryon 38* (1929) harks back to Plautus's *Amphitryon*.

Increasingly, people were writing and reading in their own language. Germany in the early fifteenth century, during Gutenberg's youth, experienced a boom in vernacular books recording what had once been oral: instruction manuals, verses, histories and legends. A well-run scriptorium – like the one run by Diebold Lauber in Haguenau, twenty-five kilometres north of Gutenberg's place outside Strasbourg –

was a good-sized business, with teams of scribes, illuminators, rubricators and binders supplying books on order to the
nobility and building up stock for off-the-shelf purchases.
Rich men acquired libraries (though there were no public
libraries yet – Florence's was first, in 1441).

Techniques, too, provided increasing variety in content
and design. Wood-block printing of single sheets spread fast
after about 1300, and a hundred years later copperplate
engravings of illustrations appeared. A wood-block cutter
was adept at producing both pictures and text in mirror
images, so that they came out right when printed. People
took to decorating their walls with woodcuts of saints. As
the wealthy became wealthier, they wanted priests to officiate
at their private devotions, and the priests needed books they
could carry, quarto-sized ones that could easily fit into a
satchel. At the other extreme, the wealthy also demanded
beauty, and scribes became supreme artists, creating the
gorgeous prayer books known as books of hours, which set
new standards of excellence.

He who wished to wield influence in Church affairs
had to control the missals, indulgences, Bibles, prayer
books, song-sheets and Latin grammars on which the
churches, monasteries, nunneries and schools depended.
Scribes could supply the need, just, but it was a struggle.
A scribe would be hard pressed to copy more than two
high-quality, densely packed pages a week (one 1,272-page

commentary on the Bible took two scribes five years – 1453–8 – to complete). What of the future, when all Europe was unified once again – could God, Empire and Church all be served? Almost certainly not. Apart from the tediously slow production, hand-copyists made mistakes, which multiplied with each copying, undermining the very idea of truth flowing from the centre outwards. Perhaps the future lay less in scribal copies than in wood-blocks, but wood-blocks were even more demanding than manuscript pages to make, and they wore out and broke, and then you had to carve another one – a whole page at a time. Copperplate engraving would have been even more demanding, if anyone tried to engrave texts. What was needed was something beyond copperplate, whole pages of metal, from which books could be pressed by the thousand, without error.

In due course, as the world knows, Gutenberg would come to the Bible. But in the early days he would not have considered such a massive operation. There was another work which, if published, would be of equal significance, and which was much more practical, because it was short.

The one thing that would unite Christianity as nothing else was a Church service that was the same across all Christendom, for nothing had so divided it. The basis of the division between eastern and western empires, between Constantinople and Rome, came down to three words. The difference was about the nature of the Trinity, God as Father, Son and Holy Spirit. In Orthodox dogma from the sixth century, the Holy Spirit proceeded 'from the Father' and thus *through* the Son. In Roman dogma, the Spirit proceeded 'from the Father *and the Son*', a phrase incorporated into the Creed in 1020. Once established, this difference could not be removed. The dispute, of course, was about far more than three words, namely power and influence and money, but that phrase 'and the Son' – *filioque* in Latin – was the formal nub of the division between the two parts of Christendom.

Given the implications of having variations in the form of worship, Church leaders well knew the need for *uniformitas*, in particular for uniformity in the central act of worship, the Mass. This was supposed to be the same ritual across the Christian world, or at least across Europe, with everyone doing the same thing and hearing the same words – the *same* words, in the language of the original imperial power, Latin, and no translations allowed. Every church had to have a Mass book, to read the right words and perform the right acts.

But there was this problem of errors, both genuine mistakes and deliberate ones, like those that underlay the current unpleasantness in Bohemia. Local rulers tended to favour their own scribes and their own local variants. If only no one had any leeway to diverge, wouldn't the world be a happier place? And what a market! Mainz alone had

91

350 monasteries and convents. This was a thought to set
ambitious young business minds racing.

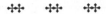

No one knows what Gutenberg was doing while Nicholas
established himself in Basel. Perhaps the two were there
together, as one of Gutenberg's biographers, Albert Kapr,
suggests, on the basis of no evidence at all. If so, Gutenberg
would have followed Nicholas's rise with interest.

Nicholas lost the case for his patron in his claim to be
archbishop, mainly because the Pope supported the incumbent. Having settled himself into the anti-papal corner, he
turned himself into the council's main legal adviser, buttress-
ing its members' anti-papal position in a bold and erudite
book. *De Concordantia Catholica* (*Of Catholic Harmony*)
argues that society should be based on an order, in which the
parts submit to the whole, the whole in this case being the
combination of Church and Empire, of Pope and emperor,
united by the council. His conclusion drew on recent history,
when the Council of Constance had ended the Great Schism
by deposing three Popes and imposing a fourth. If this was a
valid ruling – and no one seriously disputed that it was – then
it followed that the council, and not the Pope, represented the
true spirit of the Church, and therefore, if the Pope proved
unfaithful, it had the power to advise, reprimand and in

extreme cases depose him. Nicholas presented the book to the council in November 1433 – nice timing, considering that King Sigismund had just arrived in the grandest entrance of all, having achieved a twenty-year ambition of having himself crowned emperor in Rome.

Nicholas's argument is based on a doctrine that sounds astonishingly modern, as if he were foreshadowing democ-racy. Authority, he writes, should arise from the consent of those governed. In fact, this was not a new thought – it had solid roots in Roman and medieval law – and it had nothing to do with democracy as we know it today. This sort of consent is not based on votes but on *implied* consent, derived from natural and divine law. By this argument, since most people wish to be good, they automatically consent to being ruled by a leader who imposes goodness. In the case of the Church, consent is given by cardinals on behalf of all. Nicholas sums up the principle with a catch-phrase that might have been adopted by some eighteenth-century revolu-tionary theorist: '*Quod omnes tangit debet ab omnibus approbari*' ('What touches all should be approved by all').

All well and good, in theory. In practice, dissent ruled the Council of Basel almost from the start. The new Pope, Eugenius IV, wanted the Hussites destroyed, and wished to waste no time on a council that refused to do his bidding. He dissolved this one even as it gathered pace and ordered another on Italian soil, in Bologna. The council – guided by

Nicholas's legal argument — refused to be dissolved, declared itself superior to the Pope, and in February 1433 virtually threatened to depose him if he didn't kowtow. Eugenius caved in and withdrew the dissolution — a victory to the council, thanks in large measure to Nicholas.

Meanwhile, the council had approached the Hussites with an offer to negotiate. Two great Hussite generals, Prokop the Great and John Rokyzana, arrived in early 1433, with fifteen officers and a retinue of 300. Again it was Nicholas who took control, suggesting a form of words to save faces on both sides. The dispute, remember, focused on the Hussites' insist- ence that Communion had to be administered in both bread and wine, while Rome claimed you could get by with the bread alone. OK, Nicholas said, you can have Communion 'in two kinds', but in return you have to agree that a) it won't make you any more holy than using one 'kind', and b) you shouldn't use it as an argument to break the unity of the Church. This was the basis for an agreement signed in Prague the following year with the more moderate Hussites. Extremists held out, and civil war followed, but in effect, as far as the Empire and Rome were concerned, by 1434 the Bohemian-Hussite-Utraquist problem was solved, thanks in large measure to Nicholas.

Finally, Nicholas turned to a matter that united math- ematics, practicality and religious observance: the calendar. The Church was deeply concerned with the calendar because of the need to calculate the date of Easter. A thousand years before, the Council of Nicaea, laying out the ground rules of Christian practice, had decreed that Easter should fall on the Sunday following the full moon following the vernal equinox, one of two dates (in spring and autumn) on which day and night were of equal length. But the calendar of the time contained two errors. Its year (365.25 days) was 11 minutes and 8 seconds too long, which over 1,000 years amounted to seven days; and the calculations that predicted the lunar cycle were way out as well. Actually, Roger Bacon, philosopher and scientist, had pointed this out seventy years before, but it was considered so intractable a problem that the papal authorities averted their eyes. In his *De Reparatione Calendarii* (*On Revising the Calendar*), presented to the council in 1437, Nicholas expertly reviewed the evidence and proposed the only possible remedy: to adopt a new lunar cycle, leave out a week in the calendar – he suggested Whitsun, because it was a movable feast and the general public wouldn't notice – and then, as a final piece of fine-tuning, omit leap year every 304 years. This would have to be done with the agreement not only of the Greeks in Constantinople, because they were co-religionists, but also of the Jews, who would bear the brunt of revising all financial agreements. It would be the foundation of a new era, a fitting memorial for the council. Well, it didn't happen. The issue was too contentious to act on, especially with the Church in its present dire state. Reform would not come for another eighty years, when the discrepancies finally became too embarrassing to endure, and Pope Gregory XIII introduced the 'Gregorian' calendar, as we now know it, along the lines suggested by Nicholas.

Running through Nicholas's intense political and literary activity in the early 1430s is the dominant theme of the need for Christian unity. But there was another concern – his own career. Like many another ambitious bureaucrat, he was committed to high ideals in part because they took him towards the centre of power. Except in his case not quite far enough. Consider his background and where he stood in 1436 – the son of a well-off but not noble family; a brilliant mind; driving ambition, which impelled him into the Church; and then above him a glass ceiling, for with his origins he could never hope to rise to the highest echelons of a Church establishment dominated by the closed ranks of German aristocrats.

So quite abruptly this previously pro-council ideologue switched sides. The result is clear in a letter written in 1442 to the Castilian envoy, Rodrigo Sanchez de Arevalo, in which he says that it is the Pope, not the council, who is the true symbol of Church unity, the Pope who was *Sacer Princeps*, the Sacred Head. He makes no mention at all of any council representing the Church. What had happened to inspire the change?

Several things. For a start, Eugenius IV had had a bigger idea than anything the Council of Basel or Sigismund might propose. It was no less than the reunification of the Eastern and Western Churches, in pursuit of which he issued an invitation to the Greek Orthodox leaders in Constantinople. This was the dream that had, 400 years before, driven the German king, Otto I, to marry his son to a Byzantine princess; the dream that had inspired her son, Otto III, to declare himself head of a new Rome and arrange a marriage with a Byzantine princess of his own. It had come to nothing then, because Otto died when hardly out of his teens, and Zoe returned home unwed. Now, perhaps, the dream would be fulfilled – and this time by an Italian. That was what Eugenius had in mind when, in September 1437, he ordered the council to transfer to Ferrara, in the valley of the Po, which was a lot more accessible for the delegation from Constantinople than transalpine Basel.

The move was not an easy thing to accomplish for a Pope recently humiliated by the council. But there had been a shift of mood in the previous three years. Leaders had begun to drift away, and the rump council was a notorious shambles, with proposals for reform being opposed or carried by unseemly yells. As Joachim Stieber, Professor of History at Smith College, Massachusetts, argues, it seems to have dawned on Nicholas that if the various measures proposed by the council in 1433–6 were to be enforced, he would have helped transform the papacy into a constitutional monarchy, hardly a suitable position for the Vicar of Christ.

Then there were two matters that touched him personally. First, among the suggested reforms was one to abolish the Pope's power to grant benefices. Since Nicholas had several benefices that were dependent on papal approval, to continue backing the council would remove his own source of income. Secondly, there was the business of his non-noble birth. He would never, ever be made a bishop by the zealously aristo-cratic leaders of the German Church. There was only one way he could advance, and that was by sidestepping his superiors. For that, he needed papal backing. Opposing a majority who were against the Pope's suggestion to transfer the council to Italy, he joined the pro-papal minority and helped create a document that somehow bore the stamp of the council as a whole. How this was engineered is unclear, and it is widely seen by scholars as a forgery. So much for 'consent'.

From that moment on, he became one of the Pope's ablest champions, the 'Hercules of the Eugenians', as his friend, the famous scholar and future Pope, Aeneas Sylvius Piccolomini, called him.

✢✢   ✢✢   ✢✢

Nicholas now had the springboard he needed. It was he who bore the controversial decision to Eugenius approving the next council in Ferrara and the invitation to the Greeks. It was he who was chosen to carry the invitation to the Byzantine emperor and patriarch in Constantinople, and escort the Greek triremes, with their 700-strong retinue of bishops, monks, prelates, procurators, archimandrites and scholars, back to Italy. It took four months for the immense delegation to make the 2,250-kilometre journey to Venice, where they were met by the doge and the Venetian senators in their purple silks, to salutes of artillery and fanfares of trumpets.

For the next six years, the two sides, with their vast entourages and committees, heaved themselves from Ferrara to Florence to Rome to escape plague and brigands, wrangling about forms of words that would paper over their ancient disagreements. In the end, the Greeks shrugged, allowed that the Pope was superior and admitted that the Romans were right on the *filioque* business after all; they agreed to the union of the two faiths and left for home . . .

And at once repudiated everything they had just said. Absolutely nothing changed.

But the Ferrara–Florence Council certainly helped Eugenius and Nicholas. Those left in Basel had fought back, declaring Eugenius deposed and appointing yet another anti-Pope. But Eugenius had no need to worry. The old council, undermined by bickering and its numbers reduced by a return of the plague, hadn't the heart to continue, and the German princes stayed neutral in the struggle. Nicholas argued the papal cause in town after town in Italy and Germany, to such good effect that Frederick III forced the retirement of the council's anti-Pope and reconfirmed his support of Eugenius.

Eugenius showed his gratitude to his 'Hercules'. Just before his own death in 1447, he rewarded Nicholas by making him a cardinal, a private act confirmed by Eugenius's successor. At a stroke, Nicholas had leaped clear of his non-noble birth, and right over the hurdle of aristocratic canons and bishops that barred his progress. In the politest way, he thumbed his nose at the lot of them. 'The cardinal', he wrote loftily, referring to himself in the third person, 'has ordered this account to be written to the glory of God so that all may know that the holy Roman church does not pay heed to place of birth or ancestry but is a most generous rewarder of virtuous and courageous deeds.'

It was a sort of apotheosis, a vindication of the choice he had made thirteen years before, and nothing thereafter matched that joyful sense of achievement. Shortly afterwards, the new Pope, Nicholas V, appointed our Nicholas as bishop of Brixen (now Bressanone) in the Tyrol. This was a controversial act, because German bishops were supposed to choose their own replacements, and anyway there should at least have been consultation with the German king. Given that Nicholas was backed by a revitalised Pope and that he was, after all, a German, the German prelates and princes swallowed the insult. But they did not forget. The rest of Nicholas's life, until his death in 1464, was to be a political struggle with the men into whose ranks he had been so dramatically thrown.

Meanwhile, pressure for a standardised missal had been growing ever since the Council of Basel opened. The idea seems to have come from Johann Dederoth, the Benedictine abbot of Bursfeld, now Bursfelde on the River Weser. His aim, as presented at Basel, was to cleanse the Church of abuses and to centralise authority, reforms that would include a new missal, the *Ordinarius* as it was called. The task was inherited by Dederoth's successor, Johann Hagen, who in 1446 formed a union of six monasteries, the Bursfeld Congregation, which linked eighty-eight abbeys and monasteries in northern and western Germany, includ- ing St Jakob's in Mainz (it was outside the city walls, to the south, where the southern railway station now stands). As the Council of Basel neared its ignominious end, and as the struggle between the council and the Pope resolved itself in the Pope's favour, Hagen sought and gained the support of the new Pope, Nicholas V. In December 1448 the Pope sent the Spanish cardinal, Juan de Carvajal, to Mainz to approve Hagen's new *Ordinarius*.

And who should come with Carvajal but his friend, colleague and rising co-cardinal, Nicholas of Cusa, who would perhaps have been gratified to discover that the means of printing the new missal was to hand, thanks to the fortunate – I am tempted to say astonishingly coincidental – return to Mainz, that very year, of Johann Gutenberg.

CHAPTER 4

Something in the Air

Since most of the ingredients of Gutenberg's inven-tion had been in independent existence for centuries, it seems odd that printing with movable type did not happen elsewhere, and earlier. Well, it did; but without a few vital elements added by Gutenberg. Only this new recipe could turn a potential revolution into a real one.

In a sense, printing is almost as old as writing, for the act of writing is a sort of printing. You conceive of a symbol from the store in your brain and turn out copies with pen, ink and paper. It's the same principle when word-processing or typing. The store of letters remains fixed in the brain, keys or magnetic patterns, and you use the designs as references, reproducing them *ad infinitum*. It's an idea so obvious that it occurred to human beings remarkably early, as the enigmatic object known as the Phaistos Disc reveals. The fifteen-centimetre clay disc, found in 1908 in Crete, was made in about 1700 BC. Its 241 images, which have never been deciphered, were printed into the clay with hard metal stamps. In ancient Egypt, scribes used wooden blocks to stamp common hieroglyphic symbols on tiles. But neither culture used their stamps to write extended messages on papyrus, probably because of the number of signs required. Easier simply to write.

Only many centuries later at the other end of Eurasia did this sort of printing appear. One crucial element in printing is paper, invented in AD 105, according to Chinese tradi-tion, by the imperial counsellor Ts'ai Lun, who in the words of a fifth-century official history, 'conceived the idea of making paper from the bark of trees, hemp waste, old rags and fish nets'. Near his home, it was said, was a pool, where he learned to mash his materials into a slurry with a mortar, setting it to dry on his fish-net webbing. Five hundred years later, Buddhist monks carried the secret to Korea and Japan, and in the eighth century Chinese prisoners captured in Samarkand brought the art to the world of Islam, and thus into Spain, then under Arab control, in the twelfth century. This paper, made for Chinese calligraphy, was thin, soft, pliable and absorbent, more like toilet paper than typing paper. It could be used on one side only, because the marks showed through. Europeans found this material too soft for their quill pens and took to hardening it with animal glue, creating a firm, impervious surface, which, as luck would have it, could take writing – and printing – on both sides.

The idea that individual images, signs and letters could

be impressed on paper with a stamp first seems to have occurred by the fifth century. In the eighth century, China, Japan and Korea were all printing whole books made from carved blocks of wood or stone, which over the centuries led to some astonishing publishing ventures. Famously, in about 770, the Japanese Empress Shotoku marked the end of an eight-year civil war by commissioning a million printed prayers which were rolled up and inserted into little pagodas about the size of chesspieces. The work kept 157 men busy for six years. And in China in the late tenth century, the whole Buddhist canon was printed — 130,000 pages. The immense labour of carving tens of thousands of pages on the one hand and the existence of individual stamps on the other made an easy next step — printing with movable type.

The invention is attributed to a certain Pi Sheng in the eleventh century. Pi Sheng's idea was to cut out his characters in wet clay (in reverse) and bake them. To print, he selected his characters, put them in a frame, inked them, and took a rubbing with cloth or paper. This could not have worked well — characters made in wet clay would hardly be up to China's high calligraphic standards — but the principle was soon improved, with calligraphers writing reversed letters on soft paper, which were then pasted on to wooden blocks to be engraved. The same principle was extended to make metal letters: the wood-block was pressed into sand, and the impression used as a mould for bronze, copper, tin, iron or lead. The result was a collection of thin stamps which could be put together into a sort of form, from which a rubbing was taken. But no machinery could possibly cope with tens of thousands of characters until the development of vastly complicated presses in the last century.

Perhaps because their adapted Chinese script used fewer characters, Koreans took the lead in using this technique, moving on to become the first people to use movable metal type, printing the fifty-volume *Prescribed Ritual Texts of the Past and Present* in 1234. This method had its uses, but it was no revolution, because it remained highly labour intensive. The business of choosing the correct character from 40,000 or more, and then taking a rubbing – it offered no advantage in design and not much in speed; the only benefit was uniformity, which was not enough to replace traditional calligraphy.

What was missing in all this was a writing system that could be readily adapted to mechanical use. The Chinese and by extension the Japanese and Koreans, who adopted and then adapted Chinese script, could never have invented a Gutenberg-style press because their writing system was too complex.

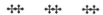

But there was a possibility that Gutenberg could have been pre-empted. Surprising as it may seem, the potential lay with those notorious destroyers of civilisations, the Mongols. Chingis Khan had started the conquest of China in 1210, a task completed by his heirs seventy years later. Along the way, the Mongols created the greatest land empire in history, linking the Pacific coast to eastern Europe by means of an astonishingly efficient pony-express system and traders who were able, under Mongol protection, to travel the silk routes between China and the West with increased ease.

Quite early in this expansion, the Mongols picked up two ingredients vital to the development of printing:

- from the Chinese they adopted block-printing and paper money, which had been in use in China since the ninth century. The Mongols issued their first notes in 1236, a system much elaborated by Chingis's grandson, Khubilai, as Marco Polo described (in the Yule-Cordier translation): 'He makes them take of the bark of a certain tree, in fact of the Mulberry Tree, the leaves of which are the food for silkworms – these trees being so numerous that whole districts are full of them. What they take is the fine white bast or skin which lies between the wood of the tree and the thick outer bark, and this they make into something resembling sheets of paper, but black. When these sheets have been prepared they are cut up into pieces of different sizes', thus creating a currency common from Korea to India;

● from one of the Mongols' subject peoples, the Uigurs, the Mongols in about 1204 adopted a script very different from Chinese: an alphabetical system.

The Mongols thus became an unwitting part of a process started 3,400 years before, when a Middle Eastern immigrant community in ancient Egypt first started to adapt hieroglyphs and stumbled into that revolutionary invention, the alphabet. The genius of the alphabet – not just our Roman alphabet, but any alphabet, the underlying principle – is that it uses a few symbols, typically between twenty-five and forty, to represent the whole range of linguistic sounds (and non-sounds, like the silent gathering of energy before the little explosion that begins the letter *p*). It is not a one-to-one match between sound and symbol, as is sometimes claimed. Its astonishing power comes from its vagueness, its fuzziness, its flexibility, its ability to record anything spoken simply by rearranging the same few symbols. Like language itself, the alphabet is so easily embedded in a child's brain that its use soon becomes automatic, unconscious, un-analysed, so that adults no more think about the use of the alphabet in writing than we analyse grammar before speaking.

This combination of fuzziness and simplicity gives it a massive advantage over other writing systems that predated it or evolved in parallel with it, notably Mesopotamian cuneiform, Egyptian hieroglyphs and Chinese symbols. These systems recorded not letters but syllables, of which every language has many thousands: hence their complexity. Though potentially as effective as an alphabetical system for conveying information and narrative, these syllabic systems were cumbersome intellectual products devised by elites – priests and bureaucrats – who could afford the time to learn and had a vested interest in keeping things complicated. It may come as a surprise that Chinese is syllabic, not the word-for-a-symbol language it is often supposed. If it were purely ideographic – with each symbol uniquely representing a word – it would be impossible to use, because brains simply cannot carry tens of thousands of separate symbolic images, and even with superhuman brilliance Chinese-speakers would never be able to represent foreign words or coin new terms, which they do all the time. But there's no denying that Chinese, like the other ancient syllabic systems, is burdensome – beautiful, effective, no bar to literary creativity, but definitely burdensome.

The alphabet – any alphabet – is a blessing by comparison, for its simplicity opens the way for everyone to read and write. Not that everyone did, because writing materials –

fired clay, slabs of rock, brass, copper, bronze, lead, pottery, animal skins, papyrus — were not easy to come by, or use, or transport, or store, often all four at once. But at least, with an alphabet, ordinary people had the possibility of communi⁄cating in writing, using simple materials like papyrus, bits of pottery, wax, even clay tablets, spreading the use of the invention from Egypt throughout the Middle East. From the scanty evidence, it was Greek artisans and traders who first took up Phoenician alphabetic writing, not the scribes and poets whose works eventually laid the foundations for literacy in Western Europe.

Eastwards, the alphabet underwent a mass of different incar⁄nations. A Semitic branch of the alphabet family was adopted by the Sogdians of present⁄day Uzbekistan, whose script evolved over centuries into that of a Central Asian lingua franca, or rather *scriptum francum*. It was this script that Chingis's bureaucrats adopted and adapted. A later version was used until 1945 in Mongolia, and is still in use in the Chinese province of Inner Mongolia.

After the Mongols first invaded Korea in 1231, the beginning of a conquest that took twenty years to complete, among the treasures they seized could well have been a number of books set in movable metal type. They thus had in their possession in the mid-thirteenth century three of the vital elements necessary for the development of Western-style printing: paper, movable metal type and an alphabetical system. Nor, as heirs to Chinese culture, did they lack technical ability, having been quick to seize on that devastating Chinese invention – gunpowder – as a terrific means of breaking into otherwise impregnable cities.

Yet it never occurred to the Mongols to explore the possibilities further. They were blocked not by technical elements so much as social ones. Mongolia lacked a written literature, and the only purpose of adopting Uigur script was to keep records for the administration of the expanding empire. Possibly, Chingis chose to avoid the complex script of his No. 1 enemy, the Chinese; but Chinese traditions were the only ones to hand to provide a model for how the records were to be kept, and for whom: by scribes, for the leaders. There was no market, no need for the leaders to reach out to their subjects, no need to raise or invest capital in a new industry. The potential which historians now see as existing in the culture of Chingis's heirs never showed any signs of further progress.

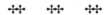

It was Korea that took the next essential step, thanks to the genius of their emperor Sejong, who by coincidence was almost an exact contemporary of Gutenberg, in a parallel but distant universe. His starting-point was the mismatch between his society and that of Korea's big brother, China. Korea, like Japan, drew heavily on Chinese culture, and adapted Chinese script. But the script did not fit the language well. In 1418 – when Gutenberg was just starting his university studies – the twenty-two-year-old Sejong came to the throne, bringing to his task a rare combination of brilliance, dedication, ambition and altruism. Advised by his own research institute, the Hall of Worthies, he revised the calendar, set guidelines for the study of history, devised syllabuses for interpreters and published the results, with the latest techniques. Of the 308 books produced in his thirty-two-year reign, almost half used movable type.

But he also took another brilliant step forward. Distressed at the complexity of the old Chinese-based writing system and its unsuitability for his language, he decided to devise a new writing system and commissioned scholars to research a range of possible solutions. They came up with two pointers, the first being Uigur, used to write the language painfully familiar in Korea, Mongol; the second being a second script devised by a Tibetan monk, Phags-pa, to write the various languages of the Mongol empire, including Chinese. It, too, was alphabetic.

So Sejong set to, and worked out his own alphabet for

Korean. The result was published in 1443–4 (just about when, at the other end of Eurasia, Gutenberg was working at his mysterious 'adventure and art' in Strasbourg). Sejong's alphabet was and is regarded as a work of outstanding brilliance. As he himself said in the introduction to *The Correct Sounds for the Instruction of the People*, 'Among the ignorant, there have been many who, having something to put into words, have in the end been unable to express their feelings. I have been distressed by this, and have newly designed a script of twenty-eight letters, which I wish to have everyone practise at their ease.' Chinese took years to master, but Hangŭl (Great Script), as it became known, was something 'a wise man may acquaint himself with before the morning is over . . . even the sound of the winds, the cry of the crane and the barking of the dog – all may be written'.

And yet no revolution followed. Hangŭl was used in a few of Sejong's pet projects and in Buddhist literature. But it did not sweep the country, because Korea's elite were appalled at the idea of losing Chinese, the badge of their elitism. Even an invention of undisputed brilliance by the emperor himself was not enough to overcome the weight of conservatism, with nowhere near the impetus to inspire technical and social change. In fact, Hangŭl has only come into its own, slowly, after 1945, first in Communist North Korea, and finally, during the 1990s, in South Korea where Sejong, always a hero, became a national icon.

The links between East and West have suggested to some that developments in Asia could somehow have influenced the development of printing in Europe. These contacts were certainly extensive enough for the idea to diffuse across cultures and continents. Nestorian missionaries, who followed the fifth-century heretic Nestorius in refusing to refer to the Virgin as Theotokos ('God-bearer'), had been active in northern Mongolia from before Chingis's time; several monks were in contact with the Mongols, including two who travelled to Mongolia in the mid-thirteenth century; and trade links continued through Central Asia. Several travellers other than Marco Polo reported on the use of Chinese paper money in the Mongol Empire. But no one seemed to consider block-printing very remarkable – after all, similar things were being produced in Europe – and never commented on printing with movable wooden or ceramic type. Of Korea's use of movable metal type there was not a squeak in the West. By the time Sejong invented his alphabet and made a revolution possible, it was too late for the news to make any difference, even if some Westerners had noticed, which they didn't.

114

In summary, Eastern cultures had a number of elements that seem in hindsight to predispose them to the invention of printing. In fact, the positive elements discussed above disguise the absence of a number of other elements necessary for the emergence of Gutenberg's invention:

- writing systems were too complex: printing needs an alphabetical base;
- established writing systems are intrinsically conservative: no one was interested in change, even if the agent of change was an emperor;
- the paper was the wrong sort: Chinese paper was suitable only for calligraphy or block-printing;
- there were no screw-based presses in the East, because they were not wine-drinkers, didn't have olives, and used other means to dry their paper;
- printing is expensive, and in China, Korea and Japan there was no system to release capital for research and development.

By contrast, all the elements for Gutenberg's invention were in place in every major European city by 1440. In that case, we may ask, why didn't anyone else come up with the idea? Well, someone very nearly did.

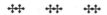

It happened, or nearly happened, in Avignon, the town in southern France where the Popes made their headquarters between 1309 and 1377. Actually Avignon was not yet technically French — it belonged to the king of Naples and was bought by the papacy in 1348, being annexed by France only in the eighteenth century. But the Popes were French, under tight French control. Then, for another thirty years — the time of the Great Schism — the great fortress-palace was for anti-Popes, while the Popes proper ruled again from Rome. Avignon dominated the Rhône, straddled in the twelfth century by a bridge whose great arches shaded revellers dancing: not *sur le pont d'Avignon*, as children sing, but *sous* (beneath). Three of the arches remain today, reaching halfway across the river.

To this centre of learning and commerce came a German from Czech lands with the *Magic Flute*-like name of Procopius Waldvogel ('Wood-Bird'). Having fled Prague during the Hussite troubles, Waldvogel settled in Lucerne, then turned up in Avignon in 1444. According to legal records, he was (like Gutenberg) a goldsmith. He had with him two steel alphabets and various metal 'formes', offering to teach 'the art of artificial writing' to a schoolteacher named Manaudus Vitalis (or Manaud Vidal in French). In 1446 a certain Georg de la Jardine took him on, promising to keep the art a secret, and a Jewish textile printer contracted Waldvogel to make sets of Hebrew and Latin letters.

Though a couple of alphabets could not have been used to print anything – there is no mention of presses, or casting instruments, or type – this hush-hush business is oddly reminiscent of Gutenberg's work and has inspired much speculation about possible links. For instance, in 1439, when Waldvogel became a citizen of Lucerne, Gutenberg's associates the Dritzehns also had business interests there; and Avignon's records list a silversmith called Walter Riffe – a relative perhaps of Gutenberg's partner Hans Riffe? Had Waldvogel heard rumours of Gutenberg's works in Strasbourg? Did he use his knowledge to con himself a nice little income in Avignon? Was he on his way to something more substantial? Or was this all a red herring (for the word 'artificial' was also used by scribes when advertising for pupils to describe their own high-class calligraphy, their *artifice*)?

We will never know. Waldvogel vanished without trace, leaving not a book, press, punch or forme to his name, only a hint to posterity that Gutenberg had good reason to keep his work secret.

There was, until well into the twentieth century, a second threat to Gutenberg's pre-eminence, originating in Holland. Here, several rich towns – Leiden, Haarlem, Utrecht –

sustained a lively trade in block-books, the sort that were printed by taking rubbings from whole pages engraved in wood with text and pictures. In Haarlem there lived a maker of block-books named Laurens, who came from a line of *Kosters* (a sort of church warden), which gave him his surname, usually spelled with a 'C' under the influence of its Latin version. For 300 years, Coster was to Haarlem what Gutenberg is to Mainz. According to local tradition, Coster made the invention, and Gutenberg stole it.

The story has somewhat vague origins. In 1499 a Cologne town record says that although the 'art' was discovered in Mainz, 'the preparatory trials were made in Holland'. Over the next century, vague suggestion hardened, acquiring corroborative detail, until it could be presented as history. It appeared full-blown in a Latin description of the Netherlands, *Batavia*, written in 1568 by a government official named Adriaen de Jonghe, who Latinised his name as Hadrianus Junius. The book was published posthumously in 1588.

De Jonghe/Junius based his story on accounts by 'elderly and respected inhabitants who have held eminent office and who have sworn and assured me that they had heard it from their ancestors'. Among them was his tutor, who claimed to have heard it from a bookbinder named Cornelis, who said he had been Coster's apprentice.

The story runs like this:

Coster was out walking in woods, where he whittled some letters from the bark of a beech tree. Back home, he used the letters to stamp out a couple of lines of text for his daughter's children. Further experiments produced letters in lead and tin, now, alas, lost, though 'wine-pots cast from these melted-down types are still shown as antiquities' at Coster's old house. A business arose, leading to books, among them one entitled *Spieghel onzer behoudenisse* (*The Mirror of Our Salvation*). Apprentices were taken on, among them a certain Johann, whose family name we will get to in a moment. Julius wrote:

It was he who proved a faithless servant and bringer of misfortune to his master. This Johann, who was bound to the work of printing by oath, as soon as he thought he knew enough about the art of joining the letters and of casting the types – in fact, the whole trade – sought the first favourable opportunity to make off. This fell on Christmas Eve [1441], and when everyone was at church, he took the entire apparatus of types and tools and equipment.

His fellow apprentice, Cornelis, was distraught and remained so for the rest of his life. Whenever he told the story of the treacherous Johann, 'he cursed those nights . . . when he had been forced to sleep in the same bed as him'.

119

Back in Mainz, Johann went into business on his own account, producing his first book in 1442. And the rest we know.

The story gained in the retelling. In the early seventeenth century Coster was portrayed handling a press like any established printer, and up until the mid-twentieth century schoolbooks and popular histories blandly stated that Coster was genuine, Gutenberg a vile imposter.

But, as historians quickly came to realise, the story is full of holes. Johann's surname is given as 'Faustus', which seems to be a confusion both with Gutenberg's chief backer, Fust (of whom more shortly), and with that of the medieval necro-mancer immortalised by Marlowe, Goethe and Gounod. Neither Gensfleisch nor Gutenberg gets a mention. Note the telling details, the friend-of-a-friend snippets designed to give credence to the tale: the wood, the children, the wine-pots, the Christmas theft, which occurred *exactly 128 years before Junius wrote it up* — a date that just happens to coincide with the date that, by the sixteenth century, was accepted as the year of Gutenberg's breakthrough. There was indeed a bookseller named Cornelis in Haarlem, but he died in 1522; to have worked in Coster's place with Johann 'Faustus' in 1441, he would need to have lived to 100. And how, if all his tools were taken, did Coster stay in business? And how exactly did Coster make his type? Experts have suggested castings in sand, but experiments show that the method would have been hopelessly inefficient. Finally, we are concerned here not with woodcarvers, as Coster apparently was, but with men expert in metalwork.

And what of the products? Almost certainly all later. *Almost* – for a number of early Dutch typeset books, referred to as 'Costeriana', are undated, and there are still those who wonder whether someone in Haarlem in the 1430s was experimenting with sand and clay and wood to tackle the problem that Gutenberg solved with metal.

In Haarlem itself no one is banking on new discoveries. There is a fine nineteenth-century statue of Coster in the Market Square, and there are no plans to relegate him to a backstreet – after all, *he* was not responsible for the claims made on his behalf. But no one these days believes the old schoolbooks, which owed more to nationalist wishful thinking than to historical accuracy. As Haarlem's chief archivist told me: 'We know he did not pre-empt Gutenberg'. It's a nice story, nothing more – at most, another reminder of the fierce underground rivalry to make artificial writing work.

CHAPTER 5

The Secret Revealed

P rinting with movable type was both inspiration and perspiration, an idea and an invention.

The birth of the idea sounds as if it ought to have been a sudden revelation, a *Eureka!* moment like the one that inspired Archimedes to leap from his bath with his famous yell. But ideas seldom jump into the mind from nowhere. If they do, like Leonardo da Vinci's sketch for a helicopter, they remain science fictions until technological advance makes them seem prescient. Ideas are seeded in frameworks of previous growths and need those same frameworks – in this case, punch-making, casting, metallurgical skills, wine- and oil-pressing, paper-making – to flourish.

The growth of the idea seems to have been a slow process. First, perhaps, came a generalised notion, an 'if only', the sort of thing that one might discuss over a few beakers of Mosel with an old friend. *If only* there was some way of getting away from scribes and woodcuts to make texts available fast, everywhere, all at once – well, just think what it would do for the status and wealth of the man who could come up with *that*. There's no knowing how it all began; but let's perform a thought experiment playing with the stages through which Gutenberg must have worked to turn 'if only' into an idea, and an idea into reality.

Compared with an inventor in any preceding culture, Gutenberg had the terrific advantage of working with a few dozen symbols, as opposed to several thousand, and with the tools in traditional use for imprinting metal. In a sense, the start of a solution had been right in front of his face from childhood. Individual letters existed on the end of the punches used to imprint book-covers and dies for coins. I can imagine Gutenberg staring at a handful of punches and realising that it would be possible to cut off the top centimetre or so of his punches, bind a few together to create a word, a line, a whole page of metal letters, ink them, press them on to paper, and lo: printing with movable type.

Just examine this, not as a final solution (it isn't), but as a stage in our thought experiment. A collection of punches could, in theory, be an advance on a wood-block, in that metal lasts longer than wood and makes a sharper image, and the letters could be reordered to change the message, but these advantages are nothing against the major disadvantage: any one page would demand a huge number of punches.

Imagine trying to make up dozens of pages like this, with every letter made by a punch-maker. You would have punch-makers working round the clock. And each punch would be unique, with the near certainty that some versions of a *t*, for instance, would look different from every other one. It takes a good punch-maker a complete day to make a punch. You would need 3,000 just for a single page like the one you are reading now. Ten punch-maker years per page! A complete nightmare, economically a non-starter, totally impractical, ten times worse than working with Chinese.

The problem redefines itself. What is needed, we now see, is a system that reproduces *copies* of punches. In modern terminology, what Gutenberg was after was something that would multiply each single punch, or part of it – each shank and letter – cheaply, as many times as necessary, leaving the original, as it were the brain of the operation, intact. In brief, what is needed is a new stage – a bridge – in the transfer of images from steel-engraved letters on a punch to printed letters. In modern terminology, the information has to be cloned – a perfect copy of an enduring original. It is the *copy* that will then produce the new medium itself, the printed page.

So the question now becomes: *how do you make a cheap copy of a punch?* Obviously, it has to be done mechanically, because re-engraving is out. Now a punch with a letter is a simple thing, but it consists of two elements: the letter on the end (the information), and the shaft from which it has been carved (the support for the information). The letters are all individual, of course, but the shafts must also vary in width because wider letters (like *m* and *w*) take up more space than narrow ones (like *i* and *l*). Copying a letter was easy – any coin-maker or medal-maker could do it, simply by punching a design on a mould and pouring gold, silver or whatever into the mould. But how do you make copies, in such a way that you can bind those copies together into a form that is both firm enough to print from and flexible enough for reuse?

This question brings us to the key elements in Gutenberg's work, the bits that actually turn the idea of printing with movable type into reality.

The first element is an image of a letter struck or punched into a little piece of metal. The metal sliver now contains the information you need, the letter-shape imprinted in intaglio. In time, this little item became known as a 'matrix', a word taken from the Latin for 'mother' – *mater* – with an ending that made it active. Originally the matrix, the 'mothering-agent', was a biological term for the womb or the formative part of a plant. It's a good image, because this letter, imprinted in metal (copper is best), is the point of origin for the type.

(Incidentally, the word 'matrix' later suggested to German typefounders, all of them male, a suitably masculine term for the punch: they coined the term 'patrix' (*Patrize*) in the nineteenth century, and the patrix–matrix (*Matrize–Patrize*) combination became established terminology in Germany; and occasionally the English-speaking world, too.)

The problem now is to transfer the information – the imprinted letter – on to the end of a punch-like little rectangle of metal, producing the same letter in relief and creating a piece of type.

And so to the heart of Gutenberg's invention, which comes in two parts: an invention and a technique.

The invention is the hand-held mould. This was truly something new under the sun, something so simple to use that it became a standard piece of equipment for type-founders over the next 500 years, until it was replaced by mechanical type-casting in the late nineteenth century.

Simple to use it may be, but the hand mould is fiendishly difficult to understand from a description. To tell you how it works in detail would be as fruitless as using words to teach someone to tie shoelaces or to ride a bicycle. No one bothered for over 200 years, until Joseph Moxon – London printer, author of technical manuals and maker of globes much admired by Samuel Pepys, among others – wrote a standard textbook, *Mechanick Exercises on the Whole Art of Printing*, in 1683. He took thirteen pages to deconstruct what any typefounder's apprentice learned in less time than it takes an eight-year-old to teeter along on two wheels. It's hard to believe that such a small and practical object would generate such technicalities. In Moxon, you find more than you will ever wish to know of carriage, body, male gauge, mouth-piece, register, female gauge, hag, bottom plate, mouth, throat, pallat, nick, stool and spring, each given its own section and array of subheads. Naturally, Moxon provided a picture to accompany his text, but even then he couldn't get across what he was talking about. When Moxon was reprinted in 1958, the editors, Herbert Davis and Harry Carter, added a sharp footnote: 'No one who is unfamiliar with the typefounder's hand mould should try to understand it by reference to Moxon's plates.' Take it from me – the coast of Norway is a doddle compared with Moxon's description of the hand mould.

Yet the thing is a joy to use, as Robert Hartmann reveals daily to tourists and schoolchildren by the hundred in Mainz's Gutenberg Museum. His performance is like a magic show, complete with a puzzling gismo – the hand mould itself – and a retort of molten metal – mostly lead, with additions of tin (to increase the flow and the speed of cooling) and antimony (to harden the metal and thus ensure the sharpness of the letter). He doesn't let people too near the molten metal, not simply because of the dangers of its 327°C (621°F).

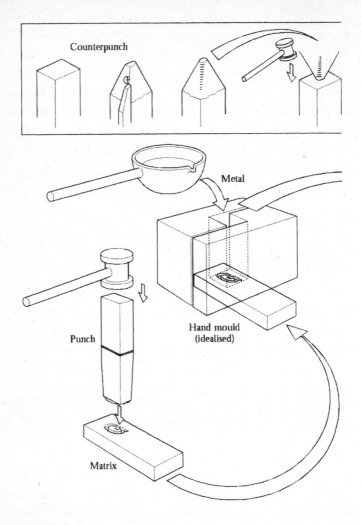

Counterpunch

Metal

Hand mould
(idealised)

Punch

Matrix

From punch to print

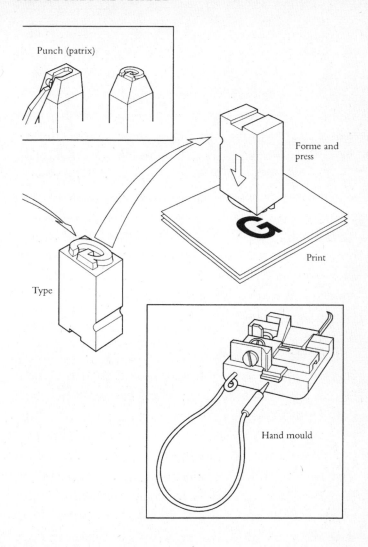

Punch (patrix)

Forme and press

Print

Type

Hand mould

Antimony deserves respect. The silvery ore was much used in antiquity for make-up and as a means of chemical purification. It was said that monks, impressed by its chemical effects, swallowed it to purify their bodies. Unfortunately, antimony is deadly poisonous, so the only things they purified, if anything, were their souls. Almost certainly this is a piece of nonsense based on a false etymology that derives the metal's name from *anti-monos* – 'anti-monk'. In popular parlance it was 'monks' bane'. Actually, 'antimony' was probably taken from the Arabic *ithmid* in early medieval times, but the story acts as a reminder that Gutenberg and his successors were engaged in hazardous experiments. Moxon warns typefounders to build their 'furnances' near windows 'as that the Vapours of the *Antimony* (which are Obnoxious) may the less offend those that officiate at the *Making* of the *Mettal*'.

Herr Hartmann is about to work his alchemical magic, which should not be spoiled by too close an analysis. All you need to know is that the hand mould has two parts which slide together to grasp the matrix, with the imprinted letter facing upwards. With the matrix held firmly in place by a springy metal loop, the two parts leave a rectangular slot, at the bottom of which is the matrix with its imprinted letter. Herr Hartmann takes a ladle, scoops up molten metal, pours an egg cup's worth of it into the slot, lifts off the spring, slides the mould apart, and out falls a little silver rectangle, just over four centimetres long, already cool enough to hold. This is the product, the offspring of the patrix and matrix, and might have been called the *infantrix*, if anyone had thought to coin the word. This is a piece of type, or 'sort', with its letter standing proud at the top. The whole opera-tion takes less than a minute.

Herr Hartman's hand mould, like thousands of others in typefoundries around the world, is the modern counterpart of the invention that lay at the heart of Gutenberg's work, or so many researchers believe. It could well have been a primitive version of this device that he wished to keep secret, that could have been held together by a couple of screws, that would have fallen apart without them, and which then would have looked like nothing more than a couple of pieces of a three-dimensional jigsaw. Unless you put it together just so – the two bits of the hand mould and the matrix – you wouldn't have a clue what it was for.

The hand mould provided the essential hardware for the printing process. Here was a device, easily used, which could produce all the amount of type needed for a book from a single set of punches. Later, expert typefounders could make four 'sorts' a minute – several hundred (the alleged but unsourced record stands at 3,000) in a day.

The huge advantage of this system was that the type itself was ephemeral. In a large print run of books, it would wear out. But that didn't matter. You could always make more letters, and if necessary melt down the old ones for reuse. As long as you had the matrices, you could cast more letters; and as long as the punches were intact, you could make more matrices. However primitive Gutenberg's initial device, the principle was the same: punch (or patrix), matrix, hand mould, type – this was the basis of Gutenberg's media revolution.

Incidentally, it would in theory be possible to dispense with the punch altogether simply by engraving the matrices direct. Later, printers traded collections of matrices to avoid the expense of punch-cutting. But you have to resort to punches eventually, because it is far easier to cut away dead metal to form raised letters, rather than to incise them. Incising was popular with the Romans, but they dealt in large-format stone letters. Just imagine trying to file smooth the inside edges of intaglio letters the size of the ones you are reading now – it was such a finicky business that punch-cutters commonly used counterpunches to strike un-get-at-able indentations, like the hole in the top half of *e*s and *a*s. The matrix remained dispensable, the punch fundamental.

Now to the second part of Gutenberg's innovation: the technique of binding the type into a 'forme'. Not a difficult concept, this gathering of type together into, and fixing the lines in, a frame to make up a page of metal type. The problems, as Gutenberg would discover, are not conceptual but practical – accuracy of setting, minute gaps to be created, text to be justified so that it looks just right. But this technique Gutenberg seems to have tried in Strasbourg, for the trial transcripts actually mention 'formes'. Perhaps it was only the 'formes' that vanished. But how could there have been pages of type without a means of making the type – the hand mould?

Years of experiment lay ahead to perfect the elements of the hand mould. Every impression punched in the matrices had to be the same depth, to create letters that stood clear by the same amount. Every bit of type had to be exactly the same height as all the others, or some letters would be too heavily impressed and others might not reach the paper at all. Letters fit together in very precise ways, with variable gaps between them that affect their readability. The hand mould had to accommodate microscopic variations to allow broader letters (*m*, *w*) to take up more space than narrow ones (*l*, *i*); and allow small letters (which typesetters would later call 'lower case' because they lay more readily to hand in the lower of two boxes) less space than 'upper-case' capitals; with all the variations coming in different sizes of type, now measured in 'points'; and typefaces; and punctuation marks – all needing their own punch–matrix combinations. Any one typeface needed up to 300 different punches, with each steel-engraved letter and every type cast from it, and every line made up of those letters, made and set to an accuracy measured in hundredths of a millimetre.

Gutenberg also had to refine dozens of other sub-technologies — the business of storing type, composing it, setting it in multiple pages, getting it on to a suitable press, making the right paper, manufacturing the best sort of ink, and then ensuring quality control to make sure the same standards applied right through the publication. As printers soon discovered, they were entering a universe of expertise and had to devise encyclopedias of technical terms.

Take two of these elements, press and ink.

Though the very word 'press' became virtually synony-mous with printing almost at once, before printing took off it was not self-evident that 'pressing' was necessary. It is possible to run off copies by laying paper on a raised, inked pattern simply by hand, or with a cloth. But experiments would have shown that parchment and rag-paper needed to be *impressed* to make a sharp image. Primitive presses, with great wooden screws that could be turned to force down a plate, were easy to come by. They had been used in paper-making to squeeze sheets dry, and these in their turn derived from pre-Roman presses used for wine- and oil-making. The problem would have been to adapt this technology to printing — to position several pages of type, set into a solid block of metal some-times weighing as much as a grown man, so that the plate of the press descended fair and square with an equal pressure on every square centimetre, from outer edge to centre.

For making ink, Gutenberg would have known to use

linseed oil, soot and amber as basic ingredients, but he would
have had to experiment to see what combination worked best.
He would have discovered that printers' ink needs to be a
substance of great complexity. The oil for the varnish had to
be of just the right consistency, the soot — which was best
derived from burned oil and resin — had to be degreased by
careful roasting. If he was already considering coloured inks,
as he would have to if he wished to rival scribal products, he
would have needed to consult artists, and thus learn to use
cinnabar — the vermilion crystal once believed to be the blood
of dragons — and the rare azure mineral known as lapis lazuli
for blue, both of which would need grinding and mixing
with varnish in just the right proportions.

Problems must have accumulated with every trial, as type,
ink, paper and pressure all interreacted.

For example, how soft or hard should the paper be? A
crucial question, the answer to which proved central to the
printing operation from then on. Paper designed for quills
and scribal inks turned out to be too hard to accept ink on a
printing press. It had to be softened slightly by dampening so
that the type made a physical indent. Every single sheet of
paper had to receive just the right amount of moisture; not
too much, or it would dissolve. Trial and error showed that
the best way to do this was to dampen alternate sheets, and
put them together under pressure for a few hours; long
enough for the moisture to permeate, but not too long, or the

sheets would start to rot; the whole operation varying in length with the seasons. Then, after printing, every sheet had to be dried; not only the ink, but the paper itself. Forgive the diversion, but as we tap our keyboards and click our print icons, it's as well to remember the planning, the labour, the care and the time it once took to process words.

That was just one unknown among many. How could pressure be applied evenly? How much pressure applied ink best? How soft or hard should the paper be? What happened when different inks reacted with different papers? How to apply the inks so that there was enough to create strong images, without filling up the little holes in letters like *e*s and *a*s? Every element had to be configured afresh, and then reconfigured as it reacted with other elements in a chaos of chemicals, pressures, sequences and timings. No wonder it took years.

And, given the lack of evidence, no wonder that experts argue about what exactly was achieved in Strasbourg. Perhaps tradition offers as good a guide as formal history. Several medieval writers credited Gutenberg with the breakthrough in 1440 – a Florentine named Matteo Palmieri in 1483, a Cologne chronicler in 1499, the German historian Jacob Wimpheling in 1505 (actually, Wimpheling doesn't name Gutenberg but credits an unnamed citizen of Strasbourg, who carried the idea to Mainz, where it was brought to fruition by Gutenberg). It seems fair to assume that by 1440 or thereabouts Gutenberg was on track to fulfil the contract he had made with his partners, and that this was indeed the 'adventure and art' of printing with movable type.

But no one at the time ever said that he got beyond research and development, and actually printed anything. That suggestion, as we will see, emerged only recently.

✛ ✛ ✛

Gutenberg remained in Strasbourg until 1444. The few surviving documents reveal little about his later life there. He was guarantor for a loan, in circumstances that show he preserved his upper-class status. Whether he actually made mirrors or not is unclear. If so, the operation did not make him rich, for in 1442 he took out a loan himself (eighty dinars, or about sixty-seven gulden). Cash flow, perhaps. But he paid the interest on time for the next thirteen years and stayed in business, presumably pursuing his research and development, having – again presumably – replaced the press lost as part of Andreas Dritzehn's estate. Indeed, one of his assistants was to open Strasbourg's first printing works sixteen years later, another hint that his invention had its roots in the city. He remained secure financially, with assets valued at 400 gulden in 1443, enough to sustain him in his long-term aims, even with no breakthrough.

He remained in Strasbourg long enough to see out the

term of his five-year contract with his partners. That was hardly a reason to stop work and leave town. There was another, rather more persuasive one: the threat of war. The threat came from a raggle-taggle army of unemployed French mercenaries. They were mainly from Gascony, a traditional source of mercenaries, but were known as Armagnacs because their original leader had been from Armagnac. For thirty years the Armagnacs had supported the French king in his struggles against Burgundy, which was virtually an independent nation in the fifteenth century. In 1435 France and Burgundy joined forces against the English – this was during the last stages of the Hundred Years War. The Armagnacs suddenly found themselves without a role, without jobs, without pay, and 20,000 of them went on the rampage across Europe, a barbarian horde as savage as Visigoths. Frederick III, Sigismund's successor as German king, thought he could make use of them, and turned them against the Swiss, who were busy fighting for independence. After a fearful battle outside Basel, they burned and pillaged their way north, to Strasbourg.

'Peace be with you,' a monk is supposed to have greeted them.

'Why peace?' came the rude reply. 'The war brings me wages and bread. Do you want me to go hungry?'

Strasbourg's citizens held off these foul creatures, the

'Armagnaken', whose name they garbled into '*Arme Gecken*' ('poor fools'). Early the following year, 1445, the Armagnacs dispersed back into their homelands, leaving a ravaged country-side and much fury at Frederick for what he had unleashed.

Meanwhile, Gutenberg had left, perhaps unwilling to risk his life for a city of which he never became a citizen, perhaps because war threatened his work, based as it was outside the city walls. Anyway, in 1444 he vanished into limbo for four years, carrying his ambitions and discoveries (though not, I think, any printed books) with him.

CHAPTER 6

In Search of a Bestseller

Twenty years previously, Gutenberg had left Mainz in a huff, as a patrician aggrieved by his treatment at the hands of the rising guildsmen. Now, judging by his actions, he had mellowed. For the last decade he had been dedicated to the very technical and craft skills that underpinned the guilds-men's influence. The old establishment was on the wane, and success depended on working with the new men.

Mainz was in even more turmoil than when he left it. In his absence, the city's debt had reached catastrophic levels: 373,000 gulden, half of it accounted for by annuity pay-ments. The town's creditors – other towns in the area – had made it a condition of their support that the guildsmen back off and return power to patrician families. It hadn't worked. A committee of guildsmen suspected sharp practice and demanded transparency. In 1444 the Armagnac threat forced a showdown. Still the Church refused to help. Mon-asteries grew fat while the city laboured on in the red. Under

IN SEARCH OF A BESTSELLER

the chairmanship of the council secretary, Dr Konrad Humery, furious guildsmen formed a pressure group dedicated to the overthrow of the clerics, who now emerged as even worse than the discredited patricians. The patricians resigned, the guildsmen were voted back in, wielding power through three burgomasters and four treasurers. Democracy ruled, sort of, except that the archbishop, Dietrich von Erbach, claimed authority not simply as head of the Church but as prince, who was owed a sales tax and had the right to appoint senior officials; and the Church refused point-blank to pay any tax on the wines sold by monasteries, or allow their clerical employees to pay any. Out of the goodness of its heart, the Church did offer a grant of some 20,000 gulden. It was not enough. In 1446 the council seriously considered mortgaging the whole city to Frankfurt. And in 1448 Mainz declared itself bankrupt and simply stopped paying its annuities, saving enough money to allow it to return to solvency.

Gutenberg was in no hurry to return to this chaos. For the previous four years, he had vanished – where? To do what? No one has any idea. Possibly there were more mirrors to make for the next Aachen pilgrimage in 1447; possibly he took his workshop and based himself over the Rhine, out of reach of the Armagnacs, in the safety of Lichtenau, the suburb controlled by one of his investors, Hans Riffe.

For years, some researchers guessed he was in Frankfurt,

until in 2001 came news that he wasn't. In an article in the *Gutenberg Jarhbuch*, a Frankfurt lawyer, Reinhardt Schartl, reported on the rediscovery of a record of a Frankfurt court case: in 1447 Gutenberg had employed a Frankfurt citizen, Hans Beyer, barber, to act for him in seizing assets of a certain Hennen (Johann) von Tedlingen to cover a debt of fifteen gulden. Not exactly an earth-shattering piece of information, but at least a strong indication, if not quite proof, that Gutenberg was not in Frankfurt at the time, or he would have appeared in person. The discovery acts as a reminder that the past should never be regarded as closed. Other documents may, like fossils, be unearthed from dusty archives to throw new light on Gutenberg's 'hidden years'.

In any event, it was not until 1448 that he was definitely back in Mainz, drawn there, perhaps, after the death of his sister made available the old family home, the Gutenberg house. Never mind the civil unrest – he needed the space. We know he was in Mainz then because in the autumn of that year he prevailed upon his cousin, Arnold Gelthus, to borrow 150 gulden for him, at five per cent interest. It was enough to finance another start-up with a little team of half a dozen assistants from Strasbourg, among them perhaps Hans Dünne (his punch-cutter), Heinrich Keffer, Berthold Ruppel and Johann Mentelin. Lorenz Beildeck and his wife would probably have come to keep the house shipshape as it turned into a print shop, with vellum and paper piled up on its floors.

Supposing that all the while he was planning a printing operation, he faced a permanent problem of cash flow. In Strasbourg he had solved this by a combination of finance from his partners and perhaps income from his mirrors venture. Now there would have to be real end products: the books. With such expenses, commitments and debts, failure was not an option. He needed a bestseller, and if possible more than one.

The Bible was not yet a consideration, for its commercial possibilities would not have been obvious. For the Church and most clergy, the Bible needed careful handling. The fount of Christian doctrine, it could also be the source of error. Indeed, the Latin translation done by St Jerome in 405 – the *editio vulgata* (standard version), or Vulgate – existed in many different versions. It needed experts to explain it. Theologians and clerics were the nuclear physicists of their day, the guardians of a powerhouse that meant salvation when applied correctly, eternal destruction if misused. Their authority, not to say income, depended on maintaining their guardian role. Only a few individuals, like Nicholas of Cusa, liked the idea of making the Bible widely available. Ordinary people – in particular the students and teachers who would make Gutenberg's primary market – did not have Bibles and would never be able to afford one, whether copied by scribes or printed. At this early stage it would have been obvious to Gutenberg that a market for such an immense and controversial project would have to be sought among the great institutions – monasteries, courts, universities. It was just too big, too expensive.

✥   ✥   ✥

As it happened, he already had a stopgap answer, something that offered the possibility of a fast return. It was the book that he himself had probably had as a student, which any student would have if he could afford it: the standard Latin grammar, the *Ars Grammatica* usually referred to by the name of its author, Aelius Donatus. This is, frankly, not a book for the beach. It was an utterly tedious analysis of

Gutenberg's Donatus-Kalender (D-K) type

Latin, considerably less appealing than Kennedy's *Latin Primer*, which those of a certain age will recall from their own schooldays. It was a sensible choice, being only twenty-eight pages long and with a guaranteed market, which he could tap into because he had the one advantage offered by printing: he could provide an error-free edition, in which every copy was identical.

It would not be a pretty book. The traditional layout was forbidding. Whether copied by scribes or reproduced in woodcuts, paper needed to be saved, so the text was crammed in, with only the occasional drop-capital to break it up.

The lettering for this textbook was the same heavy Gothic that scribes used in missals, solid lumpish letters that suggested some woven texture or other. It was this 'textura', therefore, on which Gutenberg settled for his own *Donatus*.

In every respect, except its accuracy, the more conserva-tive Gutenberg's edition, the more like a scribal copy, the better. With no other models to guide him, he did his best to mimic the look long established by scribes, preserving the unjustified right-hand margin and several variations of the same letter, incorporating the accents which scribes used to indicate short forms of words. Since this was Latin, there was no call for capital *W, X, Y* and *Z*, but what with the many variants – ten different *a*s, twelve *p*s – the type totalled 202 different characters. This inefficient and rather ugly type was to prove extremely useful. Over the years there would be many thousands of copies of the *Donatus* in twenty-four different editions. The type would also be used for printing calendars, and the combination gives the type its name, the Donatus-Kalender, or D-K for short.

The D-K letters offer the strongest evidence – virtually the only evidence – for experts to settle on the date of Europe's first book to be printed with movable type. From the way new letters are introduced, it is possible to establish a sequence for the surviving exemplars, back to a proto-*Donatus* of twenty-seven lines to a page. This dour little book was not much revered at the time, surviving only as odd pages used for the binding of later publications, and it has been impossible to date its first edition, but most would now agree that it was one of the first products, and almost certainly the first book, to leave Gutenberg's new workshop in Mainz in about 1450.

❖❖   ❖❖   ❖❖

Already this must have been proving an expensive operation. The 150 gulden loan he took out in October 1448 was not enough. For a good, profitable run of the *Donatus* and for future business, he would need more, a lot more. Imagine him starting afresh, the *Donatus* looming large, when another, far more promising opportunity opened up.

In December Nicholas of Cusa, the only German cardinal, arrived with his co-cardinal, Juan de Carvajal, to approve the new missal on which the Bursfeld monks had been working. It must have seemed a heady prospect – the two cardinals wanted not just a new, standardised missal but a choirbook and breviary as well. Surely these lines – with their guaranteed markets and perhaps backed by Church funds – offered potential bestsellers once they had been approved.

Now Gutenberg had almost everything in place – experience, expertise, a workshop, a project and a Big Idea – everything except the money. He was, in brief, an investor's dream. And, as in Strasbourg, he found what he needed in a man who would prove both salvation and nemesis.

Johann Fust, goldsmith and merchant, was one of a family well known in Mainz. His younger brother Jakob was a council member, city treasurer and future burgo-master. He himself was one of the new men, a non-patrician member of the goldsmiths' guild, and also a businessman, happy to resort to law to fight his corner. As a newly discovered document revealed in 2001 — another of Rein-hardt Schartl's reports in the *Gutenberg Jahrbuch* — he was taken to court in Frankfurt in 1446 after a deal went sour, with a demand for some 1,000 gulden. He claimed that he didn't have to complete the contract, because the deal was concluded through an agent. The court gave him short shrift and told him to pay up. He dealt in manuscripts and block-books, often travelling to Paris on sales trips, and would have had a natural interest in Gutenberg's business, in particular the *Donatus*. Besides, he had an adopted son, Peter Schöffer, who was working as a calligrapher in Paris; he would make a fine assistant for Gutenberg. Twenty years previously there wouldn't have been much mutual attraction between the patrician Gutenberg and the craftsman Fust. But times had changed, turning Gutenberg into a technician and Fust into a would-be capitalist. They might not be best friends, or mix socially, but their talents and ambitions complemented each other.

The relationship is documented because it ended badly, in

a court case, six years later, as we will see in due course. But things started well. In 1449 Fust lent Gutenberg 800 gulden, at six per cent interest, for 'equipment', which provided the security for the loan. This sum, something like £100,000/ $150,000 in modern terms, may not sound huge until you remember that few institutions existed to raise such sums, and cash was mostly locked up in property and land. Fust later claimed he had to borrow the money himself, and pay interest. Perhaps he genuinely didn't have the cash himself; but even if he did, he had good reason to borrow it. With capitalism still in its early stages, lending for interest was considered un-Christian (hence the rise of Jewish financiers). He could well have arranged matters to avoid the appearance of engaging in the sin of 'usury'.

Anyway, Gutenberg, having agreed to pay the interest charges, didn't. He threw it all into his workshop, and its products, and his small team.

⁜ ⁜ ⁜

Things did not work out quite as planned. The missal idea was in trouble from the start, for Mainz's archbishop, Dietrich, had his own agenda. A new liturgical text approved by the Pope would have meant papal control, and he must have looked on the arrival of the two cardinals with a jaundiced eye. For some years he had been backing an alternative liturgy, which was being prepared by a team of scholars in his local monastery, St Jakob's, work that continued despite the arrival of several monks sent from Bursfeld to impose Nicholas's reforms. With two conflict' ing editions of the liturgy rivalling each other within one monastery, the pressures on the community through the 1440s must have been intense – 'tumultuous' was the word used by a St Jakob chronicler in 1441. The rumbling antagonisms came to a head after Mainz's old archbishop died in 1449. The following year the new one, another Dietrich, backed the St Jakob version, produced as he said by 'venerable and illustrious men'. So now the Church had two texts, one (from St Jakob's) backed by Mainz's prince' elector'archbishop, the other (by Johann Hagen and his team from the six monasteries forming the Bursfeld Con' gregation) supported by de Carvajal, Nicholas of Cusa, the Pope and Rome. Gutenberg must have been eagerly awaiting a decision.

The showdown came during Nicholas's next visit. In 1451–2, on papal orders, he undertook a tour of Germany, mainly to impose the Bursfeld reforms. It was a sort of royal progress by a man who had become a wonder. Germans were used to prince'bishops but had never had a German'speaking cardinal of their own before. With thirty attendants, 'Cardi' nal Teutonicus', as he was nicknamed, wound his way from Austria, up the eastern side of Germany to the Netherlands, then back down the Rhine, stopping off at his home town to found a hospital for the poor which still stands today. At each town, fêted by local rulers, he preached, met clergy, urged prayers for the Pope and the Roman Church, railed against corruption, condemned 'concubinage' and did his best to stamp out superstition.

One notoriously superstitious place was Wilsnack – now Bad Wilsnack, eighty kilometres north-west of Berlin – where they believed that three pieces of holy bread, which had miraculously survived a church fire seventy years before, oozed Christ's blood. Wilsnack had its own cult now, and was rich enough from its pilgrim-tourists to have rebuilt its church. This was not something to be encouraged by a Church keen to control both ritual and cash flow. Nicholas made his ruling: the red on these bits of toast could not be Christ's blood, because 'the glorified body of Christ has a glorified blood, which is completely invisible'. In fact, on this particular matter he failed. The cult endured for another century, by which time Catholicism was out, the Reformation was in, and bleeding hosts could be burned for good and all as offensive reminders of Roman abuses (though the present-day church still has a shrine to the *Wunderblut* – the miraculous blood – to which it owed its restoration).

Among the towns on Nicholas's 'great legation' was Mainz, where Gutenberg was already hard at work. Here, Nicholas had to settle the vexed question of the conflicting liturgical texts. Mainz's archbishop was, of course, one of those princes who would have blocked Nicholas's rise, given the chance. Nicholas now had the power to take on such opposition, and he did so, through his aide, a Scottish prelate named Thomas. Thomas favoured Hagen's text over the St Jakob version, which he said deviated both from Benedictine rites and from those of the established Church. This was a stunning insult to the new archbishop, who could not ignore it if he wished to preserve his local authority. There was little recourse except force of arms, as Nicholas well knew. To forestall trouble, he asked for papal intervention, and got it, in a bull that raised the stakes still further. Nicholas of Cusa, said the Pope, could raise an army and *go to war*, if that was what it took to get his way. In late 1451 Nicholas called a synod, with delegates drawn from all the province's 17,000 priests and its 350 religious institutions. The synod met first in Mainz, then again in Cologne in March 1452. Seventy Benedictine abbots prom-ised to reform their monasteries, which included, *nota bene*, stocking their libraries with good editions of the Bible. Nicholas had his way: Hagen's text was approved, and St Jakob's prior was replaced by a Bursfeld nominee. Out-flanked, the archbishop held his tongue.

By this time Gutenberg was well advanced in what he would later call 'the work of the books', and all ready, one could assume, to publish the missal once it was approved by

Christian Europe's highest authority. As circumstantial evidence for this, researchers point to a range of four D-K type sizes used by Gutenberg later, which would in combination have been needed to print a missal. But which missal? He faced a publisher's nightmare – two conflicting texts, one supported by Rome, the other by his local archbishop. He was in an impossible position. He had the technology; he had the market; he had the finance – but his hands were tied. To choose either would be commercial suicide.

What to do? With all the advantages of hindsight, the answer seems obvious.

But the Bible wasn't the only possibility. Events abroad offered fresh opportunities. A threat was building on Christendom's eastern frontier, in Byzantium, that tattered remnant of the Roman Empire which today forms Greece, Bulgaria and Turkey. The Turks, as every ruler in Europe was aware, were a disaster waiting to happen. Turkish tribes had been pushing west from Central Asia since 990; they had been in eastern Byzantium for over a century and eating into the Balkans since 1371. Kosovo fell to them in 1389, with consequences that are all too present today. Byzantium seemed helpless, trapped by blind faith and fossilised ceremonials. When the Orthodox priests rejected the possibility of union with Rome – and thus European military aid – in 1439, they whipped crowds into a xenophobic frenzy: 'We need no Latins!' they yelled. 'God and the Madonna will save us from Mohammed!' Well, the inhabitants of Constantinople had walls – a double set, eight metres and ten metres high – and a colossal chain across the harbour as a protection. But that was no help to outlying areas on which the Turks had set their sights.

One of these was the island of Cyprus, which had been seized by Richard the Lion-Heart during the First Crusade and handed over to a French crusading family, the Lusignans. The Lusignans were still ruling this eastern bulwark of Christianity 250 years later, though Italian traders called the shots. In 1450 the Cypriot king, John of Lusignan, became so nervous of the Turks that he appealed to the Pope for help.

What Pope Nicholas promised was not practical help but cash to pay mercenaries, to be raised by the publication of those contentious bits of paper known as indulgences. 'Indulgence' is an odd name for a document that in theory united the three requirements for the forgiveness of sins: penitence, forgiveness and punishment. Indulgences – *confessionalia* in Latin, *Ablassbriefe* ('reduction [of sin] letters') in German – were contracts by which the Church *indulged* the penitent's desire for spiritual cleanliness. Once the gaps left for names and dates had been filled in, an indulgence stated that the sinner had done some good work – given alms, fasted, prayed, *paid* – and thus qualified for forgiveness of particular sins committed during a particular period – three months, say, or a year. It was a system easily abused, for priests and sinners could take penitence and forgiveness for granted and focus on the punishment, i.e., the payment. Now for the really clever part: in special circumstances the Pope could specify a cause, and for these special causes – a crusade, say – a goodly payment of four or five gulden would secure you a so-called plenary indulgence, which meant the remission of all sins. Think of it: if you die tomorrow, you have a ticket to bypass purgatory and go straight to heaven. This system, already much abused and much decried by Wycliffe and Hus, would become the cause for revolution within a couple of generations. But in 1450 it was still the accepted way for the Church to raise money.

The Turkish threat filled the bill. In August 1451 Pope Nicholas granted King John of Cyprus the right to produce plenary indulgences for the next three years, to raise enough cash to pay mercenaries to protect Cyprus from the Turks. With the principles established, the practicalities remained to be worked out: namely, how to get the indulgences copied as fast as possible, and sold, and the money collected. The king of Cyprus delegated two councillors, who subcontracted a team of agents to collect the cash.

In early May 1452 Nicholas of Cusa, cardinal, newly

made Bishop of Brixen, and still on his 'grand legation' tour of Germany, ordered his new appointee, the prior of St Jakob's in Mainz, to prepare 2,000 indulgences for sale in Frankfurt by the end of the month. Nicholas's order must have come as music to Gutenberg's ears. Here was a project that might provide a solution to his cash-flow problems just when the planned missal had hit the buffers. No doubt he would already have quantities of paper left over from the *Donatus* runs, which could be turned to a profit as single sheets. True, the only indulgences to survive date from a year or two later, but it hardly seems likely that such an opportunity should cross his path and that he should do nothing about it.

❖ ❖ ❖

At least one other project seized Gutenberg's attention before he focused on the Bible.

In 1892 a postcard-sized scrap of paper was found beneath the leather cover of an account book (I'll tell you later where it was found, because otherwise it rather spoils the story). On it were two eleven-line extracts of a poem of some kind, in what was obviously a very early typeface. This little page turned out to be an extract of a version of some so-called *Sibylline Prophecies*, a genre that had been in existence since ancient times. The original Sibyl was a legendary Greek prophetess, who acquired countless local manifestations across the Greek and Roman world, one of whom was credited with a collection much consulted by Roman rulers. Jews and Christians had *Sibylline Prophecies* of their own, always in verse.

This intriguing scrap came from a Thuringian version, 750 lines of verse which had weird origins. It was accredited to Konrad Schmid, the leader of a sect of flagellants. They were the people who proclaimed that only by self-mutilation – not through the mediation of priests – could salvation be found. Banned by the Pope as a heretic, Schmid was burned at the stake with six companions in 1369, but the sect endured well into the fifteenth century, with 300 more being burned in 1416. Schmid had a vested interest in discrediting the established Church, so in one of the prophecies a sibyl foretells of strife in the Holy Roman Empire, of famine, of brutal and oppressive Popes. She also foresees the resurrection of the twelfth-century emperor, Friedrich, known as Barbarossa (Red Beard), who would convert Jews, infidels and Tartars, unify Christianity and usher in the Last Judgement –

> *Christus wil do urtel sprechen*
> *Und wil alle bossheit rechen.*
> [Christ will the judgement speak
> And will for every sin account]

– in which no doubt those who had spent their lives

whipping themselves would escape the devil's lash. This obscure bit of doggerel is known to researchers by three titles: the *Sibyl's Book* (*Sibyllenbuch*), the *Sibylline Prophecy* (*Sibyllenweissagung*) and the *Last Judgement* (*Weltgericht, World Judgement*).

Excitement increased when it was discovered that the letters were printed from the D/K type. The type, made for Latin text, lacked a capital *W*, and Gutenberg did not get around to cutting one, using a small *w* instead. To save paper, he set the verse to run on, not in separate lines. The type was not well aligned vertically or horizontally, the right-hand margins were not justified, and many of the letters came in several different versions. This had to be a snippet of true Gutenbergiana, when he was still in experimental mode.

These discoveries turned the battered fragment into the typographical equivalent of a holy relic. Could it in fact be a splinter from Europe's first printed book? If so, where and when was it printed?

The most extreme view is that of the Leipzig calligrapher and designer of typefaces and books, Albert Kapr, who died in 1995. Kapr, who headed Leipzig's College of Graphics and Book Design, based his argument on a coincidence: that Frederick III had come to the German throne in 1440. He argued that the pro-council, anti-Pope factions had an interest in promoting the *Prophecy* as part of their own propaganda for Frederick III, who they hoped would turn out to be a Frederick as great as Barbarossa. By the time the Armagnacs, the barbarians unleashed by Frederick for his own purposes, had terrorised the city and finally left in 1445, Frederick's reputation was in tatters, and no one would have believed he could ever be Barbarossa reincarnated. So Kapr argued that the *Prophecy* had to be tied to Strasbourg and to the years of Gutenberg's presence there. In his conclusion, Kapr has the certainty of Sherlock Holmes wrapping up a case: 'I believe that anyone who considers the fragment . . . should be convinced . . . the technique of printing was invented in Strasbourg in about 1440.'

Well, most scholars disagree. It's too much of a stretch. The evidence is not there – the opposite, if anything, for the single page was actually found not in Strasbourg at all, but in Mainz. Meticulous analysis of the type by Gottfried Zedler in 1904 suggested that the publication of the *Prophecy* interrupted production of the *Donatus*, which, if Kapr is right, would mean that the *Donatus* was started in Strasbourg as well, for which there is no evidence at all. Nor is there anything to back Kapr's suggestion of a sudden upsurge in interest in prophecies in Strasbourg around the time of Frederick III's accession. *Sibylline Prophecies* had always been popular, and remained so, in both manuscript and printed form, with dozens of printed editions rolling off presses into the early sixteenth century. Finally, tests done at the University of California's Davis

Campus in 1984 show that the ink is the same as that used in the Bible of 1452–54. There is absolutely nothing firm with which to fix the act of printing in Strasbourg, and, if the majority view is correct, there never will be, because it didn't happen. Because it happened in Mainz, in about 1450–54, along with the Bible and all the rest.

So: the Bible.

It was not, of course, an idea conceived in a void. It was the pinnacle of the reforms on which Nicholas of Cusa had embarked in the previous decade, and which he drove through after he became a cardinal. In May 1451, before the seventy Benedictine abbots meeting under his chairmanship in Mainz, Nicholas emphasised the need for monastic libraries to possess a well-translated and edited Bible. As he should have known by then – because Gutenberg had been at work in the city for the last three years – there was only one way to achieve this: by printing from a single source, fixed in metal, beyond any chance of a scribal miscopy or local variation.

Not that this could have been a formal commission. Nicholas did not initiate the project. If he had, there would have been papal approval, an exchange of letters, a payment. As we shall see, at least one prelate close to both Nicholas and the Pope expressed surprise when he discovered the existence of the Bible in 1454. But there could, perhaps, have been a nudge and a wink.

Here's a scenario:

Gutenberg receives a discreet invitation from his old acquaintance to a private audience. He enters Nicholas's temporary residence by some back door. His eminence the cardinal recalls their student days and that dream that all Christian Europe – perhaps even all Christendom, including the threatened eastern empire of Byzantium – might one day sing, read and pray from the same texts. He had heard rumours that such a thing might be technically possible, that perhaps Gutenberg . . . Yes, yes, Gutenberg says, he's right on the verge. The cardinal smiles encouragement – Johann could rest assured that if his efforts are crowned with success he would have the backing of the Pope himself, and naturally, in that case, there would be a steady flow of orders for missals, choirbooks and, *Deo volente*, Bibles. And Gutenberg might point out how much more easily the cardinal and God could be served if there was some sort of advance on the sales. Ah, if only! But the expense of the current legation, taking in all Germany, is huge. Nothing more can be asked of the Holy Father at this stage. Of course, if Johann ever produces a Bible with this new art of writing, why, as bishop, Nicholas would wish his own church in Brixen to possess it. Gutenberg bows out with nothing in writing, for there would be no witnesses to this scene, nor anything promised in so many words, for Nicholas is a consummate politician; but Gutenberg nevertheless leaves with the distinct impression that he will have Church support, if and when. A scriptwriter could even come up with some documentary backing for this meeting, for Nicholas did indeed order a copy of Gutenberg's Bible for Brixen – it is now in Vienna.

But if you feel this is a speculation too far, I'll agree that it's not strictly necessary, because Gutenberg could surely see the potential for himself. It was a vastly ambitious project, unprecedented, impossible to schedule or cost accurately. But with Nicholas and his retinue in town, there could have been a moment – must have been, given the strength of his commitment – when he was seized by the idea itself, by a vision of a beauty against which all difficulties faded, a beauty beyond anything of which scribes could dream, reproduced in all its perfection as many times as required, the ultimate justification for his invention.

But he's out of money. He turns again to Fust. You can imagine the tension. Three years down the line, and Gutenberg has just about covered his costs with his *Donatus* and *Sibylline Prophecy* and indulgences, but hasn't even managed to pay the interest on the original loan. This is a grey area. In his original proposal, Gutenberg had talked about missals and the *Donatus*. Now there are these other small-scale ventures. He claims that they are totally his ideas, not part of the original agreement, and he should keep the cash, and flow it all back into the business.

On top of which, he now wants more. For a *second* workshop, because that's what it will take to develop the Bible. He has one in mind – a house belonging to a distant relative who is living in Frankfurt. It's called the Hof zum Humbrecht, or Humbrechthof (the Humbrecht house), in the Schusterstrasse, a stone's throw from his own place, and it's empty and eminently rentable.

Fust is dubious. He's not only put in the 800; he's now owed about 140 gulden – two to three years in unpaid interest and compound interest. But he has to agree that progress in setting up the workshop in the Gutenberghof – the presses, the formes and the typecasting apparatus – has been terrific, which is fine, because it's all mortgaged to him. Shame about the missal. He also has to agree that the potential is there, more than ever, if Gutenberg can make his next big idea work. It seems the only way he can get his money back is to provide more, even if it means borrowing on his own account.

So they redo the same deal: another 800 gulden, another agreement to pay the interest.

And Gutenberg is free to follow his dream.

CHAPTER 7

The Bible

To appeal to his market – churches and rulers across Europe – Gutenberg would need to match scribal Bibles in beauty and exceed them in accuracy, in two glorious, fat volumes totalling 1,275 pages. There might be a media revolution brewing, but it was essential not to *look* revolutionary, for otherwise no one would buy. There would be none of those extras we now regard as part and parcel of printed books: title page, contents, printer's logo. This was to be presented as a new form of writing, not printing at all. The risks were fearful. It would take years, cost a fortune and demand unprecedented technical and artistic wizardry, not to mention managerial skills of a high order.

First, he would need the best Bible available, to trace every different character – 290 of them, including all the various forms and eighty-three ligatures, like the figure 9 sign that stands for '-us' and the accent that indicates a missing letter.

Then he would need to get punches made. That meant a

year's work for Herr Dünne, if he was on his own. Dünne
would need help – and he got it, for two other goldsmiths are
mentioned in the sources, Götz von Schlettstadt and Hans
von Speyer. Let's assume three punch-cutters, and the
punch-cutting reduced to four months.

Meanwhile, there was vellum to order. Today's surviving
twelve vellum copies of Gutenberg's Bible suggest that
originally some thirty to thirty-five were printed, which
would have demanded some 5,000 calfskins, all needing to
be shaved, softened by stamping in a vat, treated with ashes
and chalk, stretched, dried and scraped smooth. It took a
month or more to prepare each one, depending on the time
of year. They would have needed ordering months in
advance.

But at least vellum was local. Not so the paper for the rest
of the print run – some 150 copies (of which thirty-nine
survive), almost 200,000 pages' worth, all hand-made, of
course, and top quality. German paper wasn't good enough.
Paper for the Bible was hauled overland from Italy, as the
watermarks reveal.

Next, the type. Close examination of the type reveals
initially two, then four, rising to six different hands at work,
each with their own little typesetting habits. Kapr suggested
that each worked on three pages at a time: composing one,
printing a second and dismantling a third. Each page of the
Bible contains on average about 500 words – some 2,600

characters. Six compositors, three pages each – that makes 46,000 characters needed, minimum; could have been more. No need to carve decorated capitals – the spaces for them would be left blank so that each purchaser could arrange his own 'rubrication', following a separately printed guide. To make the type, it would have taken a team of three men, each with their hand mould producing four characters a minute, about three weeks. That's flat out, with no errors, and assuming modern hand moulds. But no one had done this before. It could have taken months.

The design was mostly dictated by the scribal traditions that had produced the graceful balance of two text columns and broad margins for decorations. The half-folio page (30.7 × 44.5 centimetres) was made up of two rectangles – the whole page and its text area – based on the so-called 'golden section', which specifies a crucial relationship between short and long sides. The proportions are complicated to work out, and produce an irrational number, as π is, but it is a ratio of about 5:8.* They are proportions which, as the Greeks knew when they built the Parthenon, are peculiarly easy on the eye, and were therefore common in both architec- ture and art. In typesetting, these proportions work well,

---

* The ratio is as follows: if you replace 'short' and 'long' by a and b, then $a{:}b$ is the same as $b{:}a{+}b$. The ratio is 0.618 . . . *ad inf.*, commonly rounded to 0.625, or five-eighths. Therefore, if the shorter side is 5 and the longer 8, the second element ($b{:}a{+}b$) becomes 8:13. The ratio was widely believed to have magical properties: hence the significance of the pentagram, which contains 200 'golden sections'.

The two columns of Gutenberg's Bible combine to make a 'Golden Section' area. Its page has the same proportions, and so does the type area of this book (*Gutenberg Museum, Mainz*) because if the line is too long the eye has difficulty in finding the start of the next one, unless spacing between the lines is disproportionately large; and if the lines are much shorter they look abrupt; either way, the eye is drawn to the type, not the content.

Moreover, scribal tradition dictated that the text be off-centre, leaving broad margins along the top and left that were half those on the right and bottom, though both were in strict proportion to the whole. Gutenberg would have changed all this at his peril.

One element in the design seems to have been Gutenberg's invention: a justified right-hand margin. Scribes couldn't do this. When writing, you cannot, when beginning a line, know exactly where it will end – hence all the abbreviations and multiple letters as scribes struggled to fit texts into their Procrustean spaces, and the slightly ragged look down the right margins as they inevitably failed. Typesetting offered a chance to realise this scribal ideal by going back over set type and adding slivers of lead between words to space the line out, and thus provide an extra element of geometrical purity. But that introduces another problem. If you force the words apart to fill out the line, you risk creating 'unnatural' spaces between the words. The designer's task is to strike a pleasing balance between column width, type size and white space between words and lines.

Listen to one of the modern masters of typography, the

outspoken, gay, always controversial and impeccably tasteful
Eric Gill:

> Even spacing is a great assistance to easy reading: hence
> its pleasantness, for the eye is not vexed by the roughness,
> jerkiness, restlessness and spottiness which uneven spac⁄
> ing entails . . . It may be laid down that even spacing is
> in itself desirable, that uneven length of lines is not in
> itself desirable, that both apparently even spacing and
> equal length of lines may be obtained when the measure
> allows of over 15 words to the line, but that the best
> length for reading is not more than 12 words.

Now Gutenberg's lines average around five to seven words.
Why, if Gill is so impeccable, does Gutenberg opt for short
lines? Because Bibles were meant not for fast, silent reading,
but for careful out⁄loud reading. He therefore risks the faults
of a narrow column, objectionable, as Gill says, because the
'words and phrases are too cut up'. Yet Gutenberg's setting
is beautifully even, without being crammed. He achieved
this by using all those little scribal tricks of compression,
which we have dropped, and then avoided the somewhat
sterile look of modern typesetting with a little stroke of
genius: he did not count hyphens and punctuation marks as
characters, so these overhang at the right, providing a pleas⁄
ing element of relaxation, relieving the austere clarity of

general design with a charming variety of detail. It's a look that linotype machines and word processors cannot or do not do automatically. In so many respects, Gutenberg is the master still.

This little detail deserves a closer look, because it reveals the degree to which Gutenberg was obsessed with quality, an obsession which in this case seems to press at the fringes of sanity. For it is technically impossible to have a piece of type hanging off the edge, as the hyphen (and occasional full-stop) seems to. There is no space for it. The type was all contained within the forme – had to be, or it would all fall apart. So in order to be able to have a free-floating element on the end of a line, *every non-hyphenated line had to be indented by the width of the hyphen*, even if that particular column had no hyphen. The column width of the main text is actually a hyphen's-worth less than the forme's width. This was a practice that quickly fell out of favour, as typesetters treated all characters equally within the body of the text. What could have he been thinking of, to impose on his team, and his budget, a device of such subtlety? Who would ever have noticed? Precious few, unless they were told; which suggests to me a possible explanation. Gutenberg yearned for perfection, not only because this was the culmination of his life's work, but also because only perfection beyond the reach of any mortal scribe would persuade a prince or archbishop to buy. I think that hyphen was a salesman's bullet-point, the telling detail visible only to the discerning eye, proving to their majesties and eminences that, although the bible looked like the best scribal work, it was actually something of an even higher order – super-scribal, super-human, and therefore with a touch of the divine. What ruler, when granted this insight into the new technology, could fail to be impressed into buying?

Next he had to work out how the pages should be arranged. Because sheets of paper are folded, cut and inserted inside each other, pages are not printed in strict sequence. There was a complex pattern to be worked out: five double-spread leaves, each with four out-of-sequence pages, would be gathered into 'quinternions' – sections of twenty pages.

A crucial decision in typesetting involves the balance between the text and the white space between lines. There are several practical considerations here. The bigger the type and the wider the spacing, the more paper is required. Conversely, smaller type and denser packing makes legibility harder – all very well for student *Donatuses*, but not for Bibles that were to grace cathedral lecterns. Page size, type size and spacing were all specified by Gutenberg's scribal copy. But no one had ever printed a Bible before, or dealt in so much vellum and paper, or costed such an operation, or knew what to charge, or how many to print, or what the returns might be. Gutenberg faced the paradox that has dominated much of publishing ever since: quality sells, but quality costs. How do you balance the two amid so many unknowns?

Well, he got it wrong. He opted for forty lines per column and started printing. His team had already printed the first nine folios (pp.1–9 and 257–63) – some 180 copies of them – when Gutenberg stopped the presses and recalculated. Using the same setting, but minutely reducing the spacing, he could squeeze more lines on a page and save space. But maybe it would look wrong. He tried it: page ten has forty-one lines. It looked fine. You don't notice the difference unless you count. So he took a final step and ordered forty-two lines per page, shaving five per cent off his vellum and paper costs. As a result, this glorious creation is known as the *42-Line Bible*, or *B42* for short, even though it isn't all the way through.

That, at least, is a possible summary of a process about which nothing is known and everything has to be deduced. Experts have picked over every point, and still they argue, each seeking a share of the Gutenberg Grail – absolute certainty of what was achieved when, and where, and how.

The search continues. In December 2000, the American scholar Paul Needham, librarian of the Scheide Library at Princeton, cast doubt on the whole theory of punch-made types bound into formes. Scheide is a philanthropist whose grandfather made a fortune from oil and built a collection of

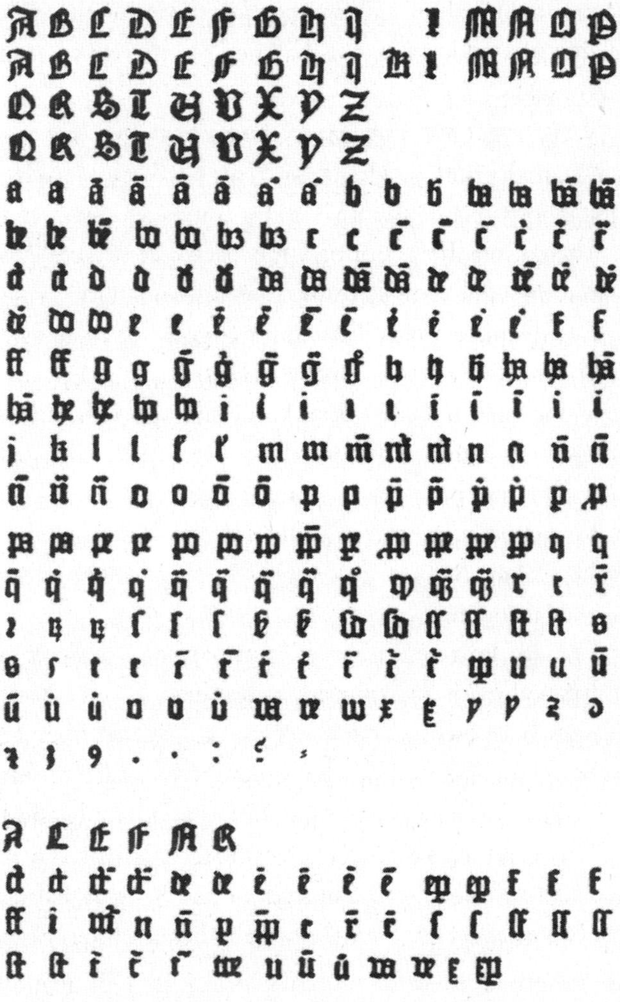

The type of Gutenberg's *42-Line Bible*

early books and manuscripts, among them the only Gutenberg Bible in private hands and a papal bull of 1456, printed
by Gutenberg for Pope Callixtus III calling for a crusade
against the Turks. Needham wished to produce a facsimile
version of the bull, and together with his predecessor at the
Scheide Library, Janet Ing Freeman, set about analysing
every letter – each pseudo-scribal variation, each ligature,
each contraction – in order to establish exactly how many
Gutenberg used. This was a challenge, because, when
examined in microscopic detail, minute variations show up,
caused (or so one might assume) by the way the ink spread
randomly on the slightly absorbent paper or by damage to
the type. To iron out this typographic 'noise', Needham
sought the help of a young computer whizz, Blaise Agüera
y Arcas, who created software to do the job. He found
something quite astonishing – that after excluding all the
random elements there were not just a few varieties of each
letter but dozens. The *i*s, for example, had no fewer than
fifty-eight different bow-shaped dots over them. Could this
have been an illusion caused by faulty analysis? Apparently
not, because some of the fifty-eight shapes reappeared in
later pages of the bull, printed by re-using the same type.
Amazed, the scholars turned to the Gutenberg Bible. Same
thing. This suggests an astonishing hypothesis: that the type
was not produced from punches at all, for why would he
make thousands of punches in order to create variations that

are invisible to the naked eye? One possibility, Needham suggests, is that each element of each letter – each individual stroke – was formed from a store of stroke-punches (as opposed to letter-punches), with which impressions were made in sand as moulds for sand-cast characters. Sand-casting was once considered a possible means of production – indeed, one German scholar, Gustav Mori, sand-cast a whole Gutenberg alphabet in about 1920 – but it is a tedious and inexact technique. Besides, the theory presupposed the use of carved wooden letters. So why use wooden letters, or some stroke-based system, when the use of steel punches was so well established in the making of coins and medals? Needham has no idea. For the moment, he lives with the paradox presented by his evidence: the traditional view that Gutenberg 'must have' used punches and formes and hand moulds, because that is the only possible answer, against the new and apparently hard evidence that he could not have done any such thing. We await a resolution, meanwhile bearing in mind that the new universe created by Gutenberg has at its centre an uncertainty that does not, yet, undermine established views.

To print this mammoth two-volume book, with its 3 million characters, was an immense undertaking. Imagine six compositors and twelve printers, two to a press, positioning the typeset metal pages, laying on the ink with their fat, soft, powder-puff-shaped leather ink-balls, positioning the paper or vellum, sliding the carriage into position, winding down the press, feeling for just the right amount of pressure. Documents mention the names of several team members in passing – Numeister, Spiess, Krantz, Drach and eight others – but without specifying who did what, and in which of the two workshops. In any event, there would have been some economy of scale and labour, with the routine stuff pouring out of the Gutenberghof and the Bible being carefully assembled in the Humbrechthof. The experts and their assistants must have made a team of twenty-plus, maybe thirty, some staying in the town, some in the two houses, all needing meals, all engaged in a fury of creativity, and all held together by the aesthetic genius, the vision, the organisational skill and the technical mastery of the man who started it all.

✤✤   ✤✤   ✤✤

The Bible, though, was only the greatest of the projects in hand, the number of which now increased under the inspiration of an event that stunned Christendom. In May 1453 the inhabitants of Constantinople discovered that God, Madonna, thick walls and a harbour chain were little use against at least 80,000 Turkish attackers – some claimed there were 300,000 – and an 8.5-metre bronze cannon, a monstrous bombard that would have done sterling work on the Western Front. Hauled by sixty oxen on a special wagon, it lobbed half-tonne stone balls at the city's double set of walls once every hour or two from over a kilometre away. After two weeks the Turks found a little door left open by retreating Greeks. The city fell on 29 May. Its great cathedral, St Sophia, became a mosque, and Mehmet, the new emperor of the second Rome, turned it into the capital of an Islamic empire which now reached to Bulgaria and threatened Christian Europe as nothing had since the Mongols ravaged Poland and Hungary two centuries before.

Gutenberg was not one to waste such a chance. He rushed into print with a calendar that was also a 'warning to Christendom against the Turk', with month-by-month exhortations in doggerel to Europe's leaders to unite, starting with the Pope (January). September calls to arms '*Germania, du edel dutsche nacion*' ('Germania, you noble German nation'), and the calendar ends with the first printed New Year's greeting, wishing readers '*Eyn gut selig nuwe jar*' ('A good holy new year') – namely 1455.

Meanwhile, indulgences galore flowed from his presses – press*es*, plural, for the headings of the fifty surviving indulgences come in two typefaces, both with several variants. What we have are the products of two different punch-cutters and two workshops, both churning out indulgences by the thousand for sale across the Frankfurt-Mainz-Cologne area. One is the D-K type, used for the *Donatus*, produced at the Gutenberghof. And the other uses the typeface that was also used in the first edition of the Bible, proof that Gutenberg's projects, and all their related activities, overlapped each other.

✠✠   ✠✠   ✠✠

With up to six compositors supplying three presses, working flat out, but allowing for religious festivals, Gutenberg and his team could have produced the *42-Line Bible* – 180 copies, 230,000-plus pages, every page demanding its own separate impression – in about two years, two furious years of work in which they were also working on the other jobs. By the autumn of 1454, it was ready.

The evidence (pointed out for the first time in 1982) is a letter written by the future Pope Pius II, Enea Silvio de Piccolomini, a man who is worth a detour.

Humanist, libertine, scholar, novelist and traveller, Piccolomini was an Italian counterpart of Nicholas of Cusa, of whom he was almost an exact contemporary and good friend. He was the eldest of eighteen children of a Sienese landowner, who liked to trace his ancestry back to Romulus, and so named his eldest Aeneas, the legendary author of Rome's greatness. Aeneas – Enea, as he was in Italian – started lower than Nicholas, had a wilder early career, but, being Italian, which always helped in the Church, rose higher. His local priest taught him to write, which got him off the family estate and into Siena as a student, and then a secretarial appointment to a local bishop. At the Council of Basel he was secretary to several different prelates; he toured England and Scotland as a secret agent; and became secretary to the anti-Pope, Felix V – not a good career move, because Felix was the last of the anti-Popes. Piccolomini's fortunes began to turn in 1442, when the German king, Frederick III, headhunted him away from Felix, bringing him on to the side of the Roman Pope.

Along the way, Piccolomini had dabbled in literature, writing a novel in Latin based on a love affair of his court mentor, the imperial chancellor Kaspar Schlick. *The History of Two Lovers* is one of the earliest of proper novels, much longer than the short stories of Boccaccio's *Decameron*. It is also the earliest 'epistolary' novel, the form perfected by Richardson in *Pamela* and Laclos in *Les Liaisons Dangereuses* 300 years later. Apart from its lit. crit. significance, it actually worked. Funny, romantic, sexy and smart, it was a bestseller for two centuries in all major European languages. The last translation into English was in 1929, so it's not well known nowadays, but publishers please note: it would still work today if someone retranslated it properly. Piccolomini would not approve, because after he became Pope he disavowed it, without breaking the habit of writing. He became the only Pope, ever, to write his autobiography.

No sooner were copies of *Two Lovers* circulating than

Piccolomini saw which way the wind was blowing and took holy orders. He was thus in a position to help Nicholas of Cusa engineer the 1447 deal by which the German princes turned against councils and backed Pope Eugenius, the one who made Nicholas of Cusa a cardinal. Eugenius rewarded him by making him bishop of Trieste, and his successor, Nicholas V, upgraded him as bishop of Siena. In 1454 he was given the task of winning over German princes to the idea of fighting the Turks, which he undertook in Frankfurt in October of that year. These were tumultuous times. Piccolomini was persuading an imperial diet to promise 10,000 troops for a Turkish crusade, while, outside, salesmen hawked Gutenberg's indulgences to pay for them.

It was while he was in Frankfurt that Piccolomini saw something astonishing: beautifully printed Bibles on sale, in sections. Word spread fast, and his Spanish superior, Cardinal Juan de Carvajal – the one who had been in Mainz as a papal legate with Nicholas of Cusa in 1448 – wrote from Rome asking for details. In his reply, written the following March from Vienna, where he was based with the emperor's court, Piccolomini noted the urgency of Carvajal's request, sent by a 'courier faster than Pegasus. But enough of this joking':

> Of that extraordinary man [*viro illo mirabile*] seen in Frankfurt, nothing false has been written to me. I did not see complete Bibles, but quinternions [those five-sheet,

twenty-page sections] of different books, written in extremely elegant and correct letters, without error, which Your Eminence could read with no difficulty and without glasses [*berillo*].

His information was that 158 copies had been printed, perhaps as many as 180. The uncertainty over the length of run is understandable, since it was increased during production to keep up with demand. By the time of writing, some copies had reached Vienna. He went on to say he would try to buy a complete Bible for Carvajal, but doubted that he could, 'both on account of the length of the journey and because, before the volumes are finished, they say that buyers are ready'.

It would be nice if Piccolomini's 'extraordinary man' was actually Gutenberg, even nicer if they met. From the infuriatingly elusive first sentence, it seems Piccolomini had previous information about the man that he checked personally, but not face to face. All we know is that someone was pre-selling Bibles, unbound, hot off the press. More likely it was Fust, taking his business interests in hand, sending off assistants to likely buyers with their printed folios, while Gutenberg oversaw production back in Mainz.

What Piccolomini saw was a few pages of a glorious product. I have never touched a Gutenberg Bible. Indeed, fewer and fewer people will ever do so, because the surviving examples are kept in conditions of such purity that they are touched only for the most extreme reasons. You can see them in their glass cases, and now analyse them with the help of Keio University's digital version. But touching and turning those heavy, stiff, smooth pages? That is for the lucky few who occasionally have to. So I shall let an expert, Albert Kapr, speak for me, in Douglas Martin's superb translation:

> It still appears miraculous that this first typographic book in Europe – and I prefer to describe the *Donatuses* and the *Sibyllenweissagung* as jobbing printing rather than bookwork – should be of such sublime beauty and mastery that later generations up to our own day have rarely matched and never excelled in quality. For regularity of setting, uniform silky blackness of impression, harmony of layout, and many other respects, it is magisterial in a way to which we can rarely aspire under modern conditions. Behind such an achievement can only have stood a personality inspired by a passionate commitment to excellence, and able to communicate this drive and enthusiasm to his fellow workers.

The Gutenberg Bible remains a unique fusion of technology and Renaissance art. If printing had sprung from fifteenth-century Italy, explanations would come easily. What more natural than for such a revolutionary device to spring from the land of Leonardo's inventiveness, Michelangelo's artistry and Brunelleschi's technical skill? All the more extraordinary that printing came from north of the Alps, only later infusing the richer and more ambitious culture to the south.

❖ ❖ ❖

Back in Mainz, Gutenberg's business had become horribly confused.

To review:

By early 1452 Gutenberg has borrowed 800 gulden to set up a printing works, in which his team is working on *Donatuses*, the *Sibylline Prophecies* and possibly indulgences, all aiming to ease cash flow while he prepares for the project that will repay all: the missal. Then, suddenly, no missal. Now the big project is going to be the Bible. But his first workshop is working flat out. Can't stop. Has to expand. He puts the problem to Fust, gets more money to set up a second workshop, supposedly for the Bible alone. But that workshop too needs cash flow, and as soon as it is ready he shifts some of the minor jobs there, in particular (as the typeface reveals) some of the lucrative indulgences. Meanwhile, none of the income goes to fulfil his contract with Fust. If an auditor stepped back in time, wouldn't he find something a little out of control here? Even if he started to repay Fust, he would have a problem identifying which profits are rightly Fust's, and which are Gutenberg's.

Here's what our hypothetical auditor might have discovered (for details, see Appendix I):

The Bottom Line

	gulden
Costs (inc. debts):	4,500
Income received:	4,000
Income projected:	5,000
Profit in 1455:	zero or minus
Projected profit, minimum:	4,500

Our auditor might well have concluded that in early 1455 there was some light at the end of Gutenberg's tunnel. Assuming the Bible sold, Fust and Gutenberg stood to cover all their costs and make over 2,000 gulden each – enough to buy twenty substantial houses. All they needed to do was hold steady.

Yet in the midst of this creative ferment, sometime around the middle of 1455, with the *42-Line Bible* off the press, pre-sold, with the money about to roll in, and fame and fortune about to be secured for all, Fust pulled the plug.

It is a grim and sad story. Fust sued for his money, a total of 2,026 gulden. Gutenberg could not pay: of course he couldn't, as Fust would have known, because all the money was tied up in the works and in its products, in particular its chief treasure, all of which was, so Fust claimed, mortgaged to him. There were hearings. Witnesses were called. A preliminary judgement was made. And in November the notary, Ulrich Helmasperger, wrote the record of the final hearing, held to receive Fust's oath that his evidence in the previous hearings was true. Or perhaps not, if Gutenberg had any new arguments with which to contend the claim.

The Helmasperger Notarial Instrument, as this corner-stone of Gutenberg research is grandly named, is a single sheet of vellum the size of a large coffee-table book, in a glass case in the library of the University of Göttingen. Actually, Helmasperger did not write it himself. It is a word-for-word copy of his original notes in the local dialect, nicely designed into a box of spidery text, and complete with a rather amateurish decorated initial for the opening words: '*In gottes namen, amen . . .*' ('In God's name, amen . . .').

Helmasperger records a vivid little scene. Not precisely a courtroom drama, because this was not a trial, but a hearing held in the refectory of the Convent of the Barefoot Friars, a Franciscan mendicant order. The church and the cloisters, standing near today's theatre just off the cathedral square, were torn down in the eighteenth century.

It's Thursday, 6 November, just before noon. There are friars in the hall, probably preparing a midday meal. Helmasperger is there, quills and paper at the ready, flanked by half a dozen witnesses. One of those in attendance is Gutenberg's assistant, Peter Schöffer, Fust's adopted son, who may already sense the flow of events, may already be preparing to jump ship; more about him later. Fust arrives, as scheduled, with his younger brother, Jakob.

No sign of Gutenberg.

Jakob asks in a whisper whether the accused is going to show up. At this moment, three men enter: the former minister of St Christopher's (the church just beside the Gutenberghof), and Heinrich Keffer and Bechtolff von Hanau, Gutenberg's house-servant and his lad, respectively.

What are they doing here? asks Fust. They reply they have been sent by Gutenberg to witness what's said. So no new evidence or arguments are to be offered, apparently. Helmasperger must have raised an eyebrow – what now? – for Fust's impatient answer is caught by the dutiful notary:

Thereupon Johann Fust declared and asserted that he wanted to abide by the day according to which he had made his arrangements, and that since he had been waiting until twelve, and was still waiting, for his adversary Johann Gutenberg, who had not deigned to place himself at their disposal, he declared himself ready and well prepared to comply with the verdict on the first article of his demand.

Then someone read out his claim, going over the old ground, leading up to a restatement of his demand for 2,026 gulden. In the previous proceedings, now summarised, Gutenberg had prevaricated. He admitted the first 800 gulden, admitted the interest, but argued that it was for his equipment, and did not have to be repaid. On the second loan of 800 gulden he was quite happy to explain where the money went, and said it was totally unfair of Fust to claim anything, because it was for *das werck der bucher* – the work of the books. No mention of what books, mind. It's fair to assume lots of different ones, plus all the related stuff – presses, punches, typefounding, paper – that went along with book production, because the phrase would be somewhat cavalier, not to say sacrilegious, if it was intended to describe the Bible alone. It was in Gutenberg's interest to emphasise that this was a joint venture, for mutual benefit. This being so, he hoped he wouldn't have to pay up.

Nothing new, then. Helmasperger concludes that Gutenberg had better do his accounts and repay anything that was not put to their joint use. And if Fust can prove he really had borrowed the money from elsewhere, and had to pay interest on it, then Gutenberg would have to make that good as well.

Fust lodged his statement, swore it was true, his fingers on the holy relics in Helmasperger's hand, so help him God and the saints. End of hearing.

✢✢   ✢✢   ✢✢

Fust does not come out of this well. History, favouring our hero, tends to see Fust as the cynical businessman foreclosing just at the moment when he can be sure of seizing all the assets from his brilliant partner, just before the debt would have been repaid. It is easy to see this as the nasty and vindictive act of, not to mince matters – and many haven't – a complete and utter *money-grabbing* BASTARD.

But Gutenberg seems remarkably compliant, odd in a man who had shown himself to be no stranger to ruthlessness (remember him throwing Niklaus von Wörrstadt into jail in Strasbourg and his court action to recover a debt in Frankfurt?). His demeanour suggests a more moderate view. Gutenberg was enough of a businessman to know that he had been steering very close to the wind these last six years (and longer actually: there was the eighty-dinar loan from Strasbourg to be serviced, as well as the 150 gulden from his cousin Arnold). Now he had made the mistake of muddling other projects in with the Bible. In effect, Fust was accusing Gutenberg of sharp practice, if not embezzle-ment, and Gutenberg knew he had a point.

This is how Fust and his friends may have seen things:

As we know, the investment Fust had made was about to pay off, most spectacularly in the form of the Bible. But that's with hindsight: when he took action, and even at the time of the case, Fust had no guarantee that he would ever see any returns. His cash was gone, and so was the income. He was in a hole, and it was getting bigger. Out of patience with his overworked colleague, he had to ensure and control the cash flow. These two were not close friends. They were business partners. Fust did what he thought was necessary, and Gutenberg, to give him his due, did not plead for time. He knew the rules, knew he had no legal defence, knew he had no one to blame but himself.

What is missing is the actual outcome. We have to infer it. In a sense, the amount Gutenberg had to pay is irrelevant, because he couldn't pay any of it. Technically, it seems, all the hardware was mortgaged to Fust. He wanted his cash back and his profits properly controlled. His redress was obvious: he would take over the second works, with its presses and its product – the Bible – and handle the business himself from now on.

Was this vindictive? Well, certainly neither generous nor imaginative, but not vindictive. More hard-nosed, I'd say. This was, after all, business, and business did not include being vindictive. He might have driven a harder bargain, tried to seize the lot. But they seem to have done a deal. Gutenberg could keep the Gutenberghof, with its single press and its jobbing contracts (and perhaps the type of the *42-Line Bible*, the fate of which is still a mystery). And, out of the goodness of his heart, Fust would presumably, after repaying himself, make sure that Gutenberg got his share of the profits from the Bible. In the end, as bastards go, Fust was less than a complete and utter one.

That was how, at the moment of success, Gutenberg lost control of his own creation, and how Fust became Mainz's second – and now predominant – printer.

CHAPTER 8

Colophon

J̶ust left the refectory of the Barefoot Friars as the sole
owner of the Humbrechthof workshop and its product, Gutenberg's *42-Line Bible*. He also might have had a
severe problem: the works were his — along with the presses,
parchment, ink and paper — but what use was a printing
works without a team of experts to run it? In fact, he did not
have a problem, because this case had taken months to run its
course, and he had had time to make his plans. During the
hearings, he had headhunted Gutenberg's most valued
assistant, Peter Schöffer, and made him an offer, saying in
effect: look, your boss is in trouble — he owes money, he can't
pay, you see the way this case is going, you don't want to be
out of a job, I don't want to be short of a master printer, so if
the final judgement confirms what we think it will confirm,
the Humbrechthof works is yours, my boy. It seems that
something like this must have occurred, because Peter
Schöffer is there, in the final hearing, as an independent

observer, not as one of Gutenberg's designated witnesses.

Schöffer would not have needed much persuading, because he was closer to Fust than Gutenberg. His father having died when he was young, he was Fust's adopted son. Fust trained him, put him through university (Erfurt, Gutenberg's probable alma mater) and sent him off to Paris, where he became a scribe, probably aiming for a career in the Church. In around 1452 he returned to Mainz, or was brought back by Fust, to join Gutenberg, a role for which he was perfectly suited as calligrapher, engraver and designer. Talented, ambitious, but with a streak of ruthlessness, he neatly bridged the gap between Gutenberg's artistic and technical obsessions and Fust's business opportunism. His skills and character served him well. He would eventually marry Fust's daughter, Christina, inherit the business and become the first international bookseller-printer.

His career displays a number of ironies. You might say he kicked his mentor in the teeth by abandoning him for Fust; but in so doing he was better placed to inherit his master's mantle and carry the invention to a wider world – with this final twist: that he deliberately tried to take all the credit for himself and his adoptive father (and father-in-law), with such success that sixty years later a major historian could write that it was Johann Fust who had been the first 'to conceive and fathom the art of printing', with only a passing mention of Gutenberg. People coming across Schöffer in the mid-1450s would have been well advised to admire his talent and watch their backs.

⊹⊹⊹   ⊹⊹⊹   ⊹⊹⊹

It was Gutenberg, almost certainly, who was the master-mind behind the next major work of printing, the *Mainz Psalter*, a work almost as great as the Bible. This would have been one of those works in Gutenberg's mind earlier, as it would have been in the mind of Nicholas of Cusa. It combines the psalms with songs of praise, prayers, extracts from both Old and New Testaments, collects, litanies, vigils for the dead and a collection of poems for religious festivals.

Its beauty is such that it is startling to think that Gutenberg was working on it – as scholars generally agree he was – while the Bible was still being printed. Its 350 pages add brilliant new elements to the history of printing and book design: two new typefaces, gorgeous capitals for each of the 288 verses, each capital decorated in flowery filigrees of metal as fine as mesh, with images sometimes included actually within the body of the letter – the *B* has a dog hunting a bird incised into its main vertical stroke – *and printed in two colours*, red and blue. (Recent research has shown that he had laid the groundwork for printed 'rubri-cations' in the *42-Line Bible*, with a few scattered capitals that are virtually impossible to tell from the hand-painted ones.) Sentences and phrases also begin with red capitals, to mimic the scribal habit of placing a red mark on all initial letters as an aid to the reader. Each verse-initial was both red and blue, in an alternating sequence: if red for the letter, then blue for its decoration, and vice versa. This two-colour printing – three if you count black – could have been achieved only by inking the text (black), capitals (red), initial letters (red/blue) and decorations (blue/red) separately, carefully replacing the elements in the forme, and then printing before the ink dried.

This astonishing creation must have started under Gutenberg's direction, but because of the break with Fust he was out of the running before it was off press. As a result, we have yet another novelty, another unpleasantness, another expression of the Fust and Schöffer egos. The *Psalter* was the first book to include a printer's imprint:

The present copy of the Psalms, adorned with venerable capital letters and also distinguished by appropriate rubrications, was so fashioned thanks to the ingenious discovery of imprinting and forming letters without any use of a pen and completed with diligence to the glory of God by Johann Fust, citizen of Mainz, and Peter Schöffer of Gernsheim, in the year of our Lord 1457, on the Vigil [eve] of the Assumption [of the Virgin Mary] [i.e. 14 August].

A surviving copy (in Vienna) also has the Fust-Schöffer device, two shields hanging off a twig.

This was the first printed colophon, the statement made by medieval scribes recording the details of the copy. Only later did the word 'colophon' come to refer mainly to logos. Actually, the term was not in use at all yet. It dates only from the next century, after Erasmus adopted the term to describe a book's final words. He took the term from the Ionian town that in classical times deployed cavalry so effectively that they swung the balance – added the finishing touch, as it were – to any battle. Erasmus used to sign off with '*Colophonem addidi*', and it stuck.

It was Fust and Schöffer who now continued with the tradition established by Gutenberg, producing a series of wonders: a Mass book that contains the most elaborate of any decorated capitals, a psalter produced for the Benedictines incorporating the changes agreed by the Bursfeld reforms, and a guide to liturgy by the thirteenth-century French expert in canon law Guillaume Durand (usually Latinised as Durandus). The *Durandus* was to be an astonishing success, with over forty editions following Fust and Schöffer's first in 1459. Other books on canon law followed. In a word, Schöffer did what Gutenberg had hoped to do – provide a hungry Church with the books it needed.

So now, quite quickly, Gutenberg risked being written out of his own creation. In a sense he never recovered after the break with Fust. He stopped paying interest on the eighty dinars he borrowed from St Thomas's, Strasbourg, in 1442. Writs were served, threats of arrest made. As a citizen of Mainz, which did not recognise Strasbourg's jurisdiction, he could afford to ignore them, but it was enough to send any normal sixty-year-old into terminal depression.

But Gutenberg never played the victim. He witnessed a property sale in 1457, showing he remained in Mainz, along with his 'honourable and discreet' co-witnesses. And he kept the Gutenberghof (as almost all researchers now agree, after decades of wrangling over what might have or 'must have' happened). Other publications followed, all in the D-K type, and all providing evidence of his involve-ment: many more *Donatuses*, three other calendars, a papal appeal for a Turkish crusade (the one analysed by Need-ham), a list of archbishoprics, a single-page prayer (of which only one example survives: it has a nail-hole in the top, showing that its pious owner had hung it up in his home). There is continuity of policy here, additional evidence that he was still at work at the Gutenberghof.

This was just the start of a fighting comeback. He was, I imagine, seething at what had been lost, and determined to claw back what he could. The *42-Line Bible* was on sale, and there was no shortage of demand for his products and skills, and his own trainees were beginning to branch out on their own. In around 1457 Heinrich Eggestein, a former priest from Strasbourg who had probably worked with Gutenberg in Mainz, returned to Strasbourg to set up his own works with his partner, Johann Mentelin. The following year, there arrived in Mainz a Frenchman, Nicholas Jenson, a painter and coin-engraver who had been ordered by the French king, Charles VII, to learn the art of printing from Gutenberg and return with his new skill. Realising what he had unleashed, driven by undimmed ambition, with unrivalled expertise and experience, all he needed to re-establish himself was – as always – finance.

He found it in the unlikely person of Mainz's town clerk, Dr Konrad Humery, whom we first heard of as head of the group set up to counter the dire influence of the clerics. It was Humery's backing that enabled Gutenberg to follow up an intriguing offer from Bamberg, 150 kilometres to the east.

The story of what happened, like so much in Gutenberg's life, is not stated in any written source; it has to be derived by much argument from the evidence, in this case thirteen surviving copies and some odd fragments of a Bible set in columns of thirty-six lines, which expands the work by about twenty per cent to 1,768 pages. The *36-Line Bible* – the *B36* – uses a revised version of the old D-K type, which together with compositors' quirks and ink analysis, pretty much proves that it was typeset in Mainz. But watermarks in the paper indicate that it was printed in Bamberg. How is this to be explained?

The most likely sequence of events is as follows:

The secretary to the bishop of Bamberg was Albrecht Pfister. Pfister knew Helmasperger, who doubled as secretary to the bishop. In 1459 Bamberg acquired a new bishop, Georg von Schaumburg, a prince in his own right, extremely rich and a connoisseur, who wanted a Bible of his own. But by the time he took office, all the *42-Line Bibles* were sold. So the bishop commissioned a completely new edition, perhaps some eighty copies in all, twenty on vellum, sixty on paper. The decision changed Pfister's life, because it was he who organised the printing, setting up his own print shop with Gutenberg's type and the help of his team – four of them, probably. Pfister acquired the type and went on to print a *Donatus* and some other popular works, which combined text and woodcut illustrations. He would never match Gutenberg in expertise, but his workshop would train several men who later helped establish the new industry in Italy.

First Strasbourg, now Bamberg: Gutenberg's invention, like a living thing, was beginning to lay down roots outside his home town.

Back in Mainz, it seems likely that Gutenberg was already working on his next big idea, which was to repeat the success of the *Donatus* with another standard reference work, a Latin encyclopedia known as the *Catholicon*. This work poses a mass of problems for researchers, who once again have had to wrestle with conflicting evidence and arguments. The book, a combined dictionary and grammar in 1,500 formidable pages, had been compiled 200 years before by a Genoese friar, Giovanni Balbi. It was, like the *Donatus*, a work of mind-numbing tedium, but full of information, much copied and much in demand among studious clerics. There was a technical problem: to devise a tiny typeface that would squeeze the whole encyclopedia into half the space.

The *Catholicon* duly appeared in 1460. Its 746 pages, set in the smallest print devised to that date, contained *5 million characters*, almost twice the length of the Bible. The type, in a style favoured by scribes for non-liturgical texts, is an early form of Roman, which is both much more legible to modern eyes and also resembles some of Gutenberg's other publications. On the other hand it was, by comparison with the Bibles, a bit rough, with ragged right-hand margins. Researchers wondered whether the meticulous Gutenberg could really have been responsible for it.

Doubts increased when a paper researcher showed that the *Catholicon* appeared in three different editions, probably over more than a decade, during which period Gutenberg left Mainz, resettled and eventually died. That meant it had to have been printed in at least two different places years apart, which raised a whole new set of problems. Was it really credible that Gutenberg and/or the team that inherited the *Catholicon* type worked with, stored and transported 5 million characters, all set in 746 formes, each weighing 10 kilogrames apiece? That's seven tonnes of metal to cart about – unless the pages were not set in type at all, as the American expert Paul Needham suggested in the 1980s. Needham argued that the whole work could have been cast in two-line slugs of metal, which could have been taken apart and reconstituted far more easily. But in that case Gutenberg had also to be seen as the inventor of a totally new process: stereotyping.

The arguments are extremely technical, and no one has yet made complete sense of the evidence. The consensus is that the *Catholicon* was set in type, and that Gutenberg was indeed behind it. But the enigma endures, exemplified by an extensive colophon.

This dedicates the work to God 'at whose bidding the tongues of infants [perhaps here with the fundamental sense of "speechless ones"] become eloquent, and who often reveals to the lowly what he conceals to the wise'. It also boasts mightily about its origins in glorious Mainz in 'the year of our Lord's incarnation 1460'; and makes much of its production 'without help of reed, stylus or quill, but by a wonderful concord, proportion and measure of punches and formes'.

This is a puzzle. It is proudly nationalistic, assertively

traditional, explicit about its use of printing – and with no clue to authorship. It displays a literary flair, echoing biblical phrases: He that hath ears to hear, let him hear; Out of the mouths of babes and sucklings. It also has an echo of Nicholas of Cusa's doctrine of *docta ignorantia*: 'I was led to the learning that is ignorance to grasp the incomprehensible.' There is a deliberate quality here that encourages interpreta-tion. What if Gutenberg is covering his tracks with a show of modesty that is not as disingenuous as it looks? What if he is coming out in discreet opposition to Fust and Schöffer, asserting traditional values against their brash modernity, using the new device of a printer's statement to attribute his invention to God's grace, casting himself in the role of the passive medium, proud of his 'lowly' anonymity, in contrast to his egotistical, self-serving ex-partners? Would not this be a subtle form of revenge?

⁜ ⁜ ⁜

Assuming the *Catholicon* was printed in Mainz in its early versions, it turned out to be the last major work in which Gutenberg was directly involved, because in 1462 Mainz's troubles came to a violent and terrifying climax. Of all the setbacks he had experienced – flight from Mainz's civil strife in his youth, Andreas Dritzehn's death, flight from Strasbourg, the dispute with Fust – this was the nastiest, and certainly the closest that Gutenberg came to violent death.

The cause of the trouble was the old dispute between those who thought councils should be the ultimate fount of Christian authority, and those who thought the Pope should. In Germany this was a fraught issue, because every church leader had to pay a tax when he was confirmed in office by the Pope – 10,000 gulden in the case of Mainz's archbishop – a policy that was understandably unpopular with anti-papal conciliarists. The papal party had regained a good deal of ground, thanks to Nicholas of Cusa and his papal backers, of whom the latest was his old colleague, Enea Sylvio Piccolomini, now Pope Pius II. In Germany those keen to see papal influence limited by councils wanted to convene another, a task that would normally be undertaken by the Empire's senior prelate, the archbishop of Mainz.

In June 1459 Mainz got a new archbishop, just – he secured his position by a single vote, thanks to papal support. But Pius exacted a price: the new man, Diether von Isenburg by name, had to promise to go to war with the anti-papal, pro-conciliar ruler of the Rhineland, his co-elector, Frederick. This was Pius's smart way of setting elector against elector, thus undermining imperial unity and extending his own authority. Diether did his unwilling best, picked a quarrel, took his army to war, made a poor job of it, suffering defeat in July 1460, and was glad to make peace with his countryman.

Now one thing led to another in a string of causes and effects, spiralling from the petty to the vicious to the deadly. Diether still had to have his election confirmed. This Pius said he would give in exchange for further assurances: Diether was to promise never *ever* to call a council, and also to hand over a tenth of his income for the coming crusade against the Turks. This proved one demand too many. Diether refused, sent a delegation to lodge an appeal and won a reprieve. He could have a year to pay up, Pius ruled, as long as the delegates paid the tax due on Diether's accession then and there. Ten thousand gulden, the traditional amount, was a lot to find on the spur of the moment, but within reach. And then another shock: Pius arbitrarily doubled the fee to 20,000 gulden. To pay, the delegates had to take out a loan – from a local lender approved by the Vatican, of course. In the small print of the loan contract was an interesting clause: default meant excommunication for Diether.

Diether sent a horrified retraction and, by the terms of a deal to which he was not signed up, was promptly excommunicated.

Furious, he summoned the imperial electors to a meeting in Nuremberg in early 1461. Bishops, archbishops, electors and princes agreed that it was intolerable that the Pope should so 'burden and oppress the whole German nation'. It had to stop. There would be no more payments to Rome.

There would be councils. The Pope would be controlled.

Pius counterattacked (it's hard to remember that this is Piccolomini, our brilliant and witty author, now struggling to cope with the burdens of high office). He dispatched delegates whose job was to meet leaders – one being Adolf von Nassau, the very man defeated in the archiepiscopal elections – and make concessions. The policy worked, mainly because the German king could not contemplate all-out war between Pope and Empire and had no option but to refuse backing for Diether. At the same time, the papal delegates had made Diether's rival, Adolf, an offer of support. Diether would be removed, Adolf von Nassau installed. An order to this effect was signed by the Pope in August 1461 and rushed into Adolf's eager hands, with strict orders to preserve secrecy, while more reassurances went out to the German princes that no one would force them to pay taxes without their consent. It was enough to secure their neutrality in the coming struggle.

The climax to this act of the drama came in the cathedral chapterhouse – now the museum – on 26 September. All Mainz's leaders were summoned to hear what Pius had decided. Diether was there, and Adolf, and the cathedral canons, and other dignitaries, including the two papal legates. Adolf himself stepped forward and read out the papal bull firing the incumbent and elevating himself. After a stunned silence, the canons withdrew to consider. Another long pause, before the only possible conclusion – that canon law supported Pius's action. Diether was out, Adolf the new prince-archbishop.

Diether was apparently without redress, when out of the blue his old enemy and now his ally, Frederick, offered his army. Diether's spirits rallied. He promised his dithering adversaries, the guildsmen, that they would suffer wrongs no more at the hands of clerics if they backed him. No more privileges or tax exemptions for the clergy: it was what the guildsmen had been demanding for years. The city council, which until now had been as transfixed as deer caught in headlights, swung behind Diether, swayed by the prince's new adviser, none other than the anti-clerical Konrad Humery, Gutenberg's financier and thus co-owner in all probability of the Gutenberghof printing works.

Once again, the screws tightened. In February 1462 the Pope ordered every local prelate in the Empire to proclaim Diether's anathema, that curse with bell, book and candle by which 'we separate him from the precious body and blood of the Lord . . . we judge him damned until he shall return to amendment and to penitence'. In every pulpit, the dire words were uttered. But not in Mainz.

And now the printers entered the scene. That August, Fust and Schöffer rushed out the emperor's condemnation of Diether, hotly followed by Pius's own rejection of Diether and his replacement by Adolf. In response, Diether and

Humery published a manifesto, possibly through Gutenberg, suggesting arbitration (no takers, apparently). Other pamphlets came from Adolf's side, then from Diether's. Both sets of printers, it seems, were determined not to appear partisan in this propaganda war, but to act purely as businessmen, rivalling only each other, so that they could pick up contracts without prejudice.

In June 1462 Elector Frederick, Diether's ally, brought his army towards Mainz. Adolf confronted him at Seckenheim, near Schwetzingen, and lost. In Mainz, Diether became the people's darling. The townsfolk prepared for war – not that they could do much, because the coffers were, as always, practically empty. When offered some 200 mounted mercenaries by Frederick, the burgomasters wrung their hands, said they had nothing to pay with and declined. Diether was astounded by their short-sightedness: 'You say you are behind me, but you do nothing!' War was coming and they worried about their *accounts*!

Outside the walls, Adolf's supporters gathered – 1,000 horsemen, 2,000 foot-soldiers and 400 Swiss mercenaries. Disreputable robber barons, like 'Black Duke' Ludwig von Veldenz and Albig von Sulz, haggled over how to share out the booty – wine, grain, crops, weapons, jewellery, cash, domestic goods. Lesser warlords were promised 5,000 gulden apiece. Whoever was over the walls first would get 1,000 gulden and a town house. These were not people who would bring much credit to the Pope, whose decision they were supposedly supporting.

In Mainz, fear spread. Elector Frederick, warned of the coming assault, steered clear. A few guildsmen, eager to see the city's patrician and clerical bosses brought low, planned treachery. A labourer, Heinz, and a fisherman named Dude were said to have bribed watchmen to leave unlocked a gate down in the south-west corner, a distant spot shielded from view by orchards and vineyards.

The attack came before dawn on 28 October. By flickering torchlight, foot-soldiers circled the walls, seeking a soft spot. Near the Gautor (District Gate), close to where the walls of St Jakob's loomed against the eastern sky, soldiers pushed wheeled scaling ladders up against the wall − you can see one of the ladders in the town museum today − and swarmed over into the shadowy orchards. As the bell of St Quentin's clanged the alarm, and men struggled into armour and ran to the walls, the Gautor Gate was flung open, and Adolf's troops streamed in, advancing down the Gaustrasse with yells of 'Kill the heretics!' Three hundred citizens formed up in the centre behind a flag and two cannons. Diether fled in the other direction, over the walls and across the Rhine, promising reinforcements that never came. In the strengthening daylight, the battle exploded across the town, as little groups − one led by Fust's younger brother, Jakob − skirmished along side streets. By nightfall,

400 citizens were dead, among them Jakob, leaving Adolf's men plundering at will through the big stone and timber houses of the patricians, the clergy and the Jews.

Next day, Adolf von Nassau rode in past the fires and corpses to claim his position as rightful archbishop. All citizens were ordered to the market square by the cathedral, where, the following morning, 30 October, 800 gathered, expecting to have to swear loyalty to their new lord. They found themselves surrounded by troops, the Swiss with cross-bows loaded and ready to fire, the Germans with swords and pikes. They were penned (as a chronicler recorded) like sheep, and just as helpless. Adolf addressed them: for their disobedience to the Pope and emperor, he should kill them; but he would be merciful, and only fine them and banish them. There lay their way – along the Gaustrasse to the Gautor, where the invaders had burst through two days before.

No time to gather possessions. Anyone who could have fought, anyone with a claim to eminence was expelled with their families, passing between lines of grim soldiers yelling insults. At the gate, they filed through in pairs, their names being recorded by scribes, and allowed to pass only when they had paid half a gulden. With them, almost certainly, was Gutenberg, who, to any of Adolf's supporters in the know, would have been highly suspect as a colleague of Diether's secretary, Humery.

Adolf took everything: the cash from the treasury (not much), cloth, art treasures, furniture, clothes. Every commander received his promised 5,000 gulden, every horseman fifteen gulden, every foot-soldier seven and a half. All the city's debts were written off. Total losses were later set at 2 million gulden, 10,000 times the amount the burgomasters had saved by refusing to pay for mercenaries. Mainz became a ghost town for the next six months.

After a winter spent shivering in outlying villages and estates, some of the exiles were allowed to return. Others, about 400, were made to take an oath that they would never again in their lives approach within a kilometre of the city (actually, since this was before kilometres, the terms specified a German *Meile*, from the Latin *mille passus*, 1,000 paces, i.e. not a statute mile, but something closer to a kilometre).

A year later, Adolf, with the emperor's approval, proclaimed a new law banning electors and princes from meeting without imperial approval. That was the end of the conciliar movement and its vague foreshadowings of democracy, for . . . well, we will see how long in a later chapter. Traditional authority was back in harness, the guilds dissolved. In a glittering ceremony in Frankfurt, Diether renounced his title, handing over his electoral sword to a papal legate, in return for suitable compensation. In Mainz, Fust and Schöffer were back in business, happily doing the Pope's work: in 1463 they published a papal bull against the 'despicable infidel Turks'.

Gutenberg never again lived in Mainz. His house was seized and leased to one of Adolf's men. He and his team would not have been able to take anything much with them, except perhaps a few tools and punches. It must have seemed the end of everything for which he had struggled for the last thirty years.

That was the surface reality. Underneath, though, something new had grown, and Mainz's catastrophic little war, which seemed to end with conservatism supreme, in fact ensured the release and scattering of the seeds of revolution. Heinrich Eggestein was already back in Strasbourg, at his own printing shop with Johann Mentelin. Others now headed out to join Pfister in Bamberg, to Basel, to Cologne, and across the Alps to Italy.

Banned from Mainz, and now at some small risk of arrest from the bailiffs of St Thomas's in Strasbourg, Gutenberg returned to the only other place his family had roots, Eltville. His niece had a house there, and so did patrician friends, the Bechtermünzes, whom he had known as a child.

Here, it seems, he re-established himself in printing, thanks not only to Humery's finance but also to Heinrich and Nicolaus Bechtermünz, who provided the space. The site of the press is still there, at the heart of Eltville's impossibly charming huddle of cobblestones and half-timbering. It's a few minutes' walk from the river and the broad embankment, where in summer tourists stroll among plane trees, waiting for ferries to Mainz, Cologne and Düsseldorf. Above the fore-shore looms the Electoral Castle, the archbishop's residence and Eltville's shield, with its white tower and fairy-tale turrets. Behind the castle, overlooking its ramparts, is the Gensfleisch house. And right round the corner is the old Bechtermünz place, three storeys of grey stone, with eyebrow dormers in its steep, tiled roof. Today, it's a wine cellar and restaurant, run by the Koeglers for four generations. Gutenberg would recognise it still, for the past is part of the present, in the name – 'H. Bechtermünz' – picked out in arching metal over the gateway, and in the wine presses, which were, after all, in essence printing presses.

There is no proof of Gutenberg's direct involvement, but researchers agree that it must be more than coincidence that a new printing works should arise in little Eltville, Gutenberg's second home, so soon after he was expelled from his main one. He is reckoned to have been behind an indulgence printed in 1464 to raise money to free Christians in foreign captivity. It was in the *Catholicon* type, the one that in the late 1450s was owned by Gutenberg and his backer, Humery. It seems likely that the punches at least could have been brought downriver from the Gutenberghof. And from 1465–7 there appeared a Latin dictionary, probably an abridgement of part of the *Catholicon*, known as the *Vocabularius ex quo* (from its opening two words: 'From what . . .').

At last, well into his sixties, Gutenberg was acknowledged. As part of his policy of making peace in his new realm, Adolf remembered the man who had helped make propaganda in the civil war, and who might make more unless he and his powerful invention were brought onside. Besides, by now it would have become clear that Rome itself was more than a little interested in printing, and Adolf owed Rome everything.

In January 1465 he awarded the old inventor a pension-in-kind, in effect granting him the trappings of knighthood, telling him of the award in flattering terms:

> We have recognised the agreeable and willing service which our dear, faithful Johann Gutenberg has rendered, and may and shall render in the future . . . We shall, each and every year, when we clothe our ordinary courtiers, clothe him at the same time like one of our noblemen.

Gutenberg was also to be granted 2,000 kilograms of grain and 2,000 litres of wine a year, enough for a substantial household, and to be exempt from tax, all in exchange for his loyalty, sworn by oath. This was a complete pardon, with additional benefits, on the understanding that his printing press would be there for Adolf's use, should he wish. Gutenberg was free to come and go in Mainz, free of want, and free of fear of arrest by Strasbourg bailiffs.

It was a sort of vindication, to be honoured like this, even if the reasons were transparently political, and to know that his invention was taking the world by storm. And what would have been his reaction, I wonder, when in 1466 he heard that his old adversary Fust, while on a sales trip to Paris, had caught the plague and died, leaving Schöffer as sole heir to the business?

⚜ ⚜ ⚜

Gutenberg's death happened without fuss. Years later, some-one – probably Eltville's priest, Leonhard Mengoss – bought a book printed with the new technology in 1470, remem-bered the man who had started it all, and scribbled in it: 'AD 1468, on St Blasius' Day [3 February] died the honoured master Henne Ginsfleiss [for Gutenberg was also known as Gensfleisch, and still is in Eltville] on whom God have mercy.' It's the only evidence we have of the date of his death.

Three weeks later his backer and colleague, Konrad Humery, took over the equipment of the Eltville press, which technically belonged to him anyway. But by now this was more than equipment. There were political implications. In assuming possession of Gutenberg's professional effects, he made an undertaking, written for Adolf's eyes, by which he promised to use these explosive objects, this army of little metal soldiers, to print only in Mainz and, if he sold up, to sell only to a citizen of Mainz. He had little chance to do much with his equipment, though. He died two years later.

Gutenberg was buried, according to a record made by his distant cousin, Adam Gelthus, in St Francis' Church, the same Convent of the Barefoot Friars where thirteen years before he had been deprived of the fruits of his labour.

> *In memory of the inventor of the art of printing*
> *D.O.M.S.* [*Deo Optimo Maximo Sacrum*: Sacred to God in the Highest]
> To Johann Gensfleisch
> Inventor of the art of printing
> Deserver of the best from all nations and tongues
> To the immortal memory of his name
> Adam Gelthus places [this memorial].
> His remains rest peacefully
> In the church of St Francis, Mainz.

Gelthus's written record, included without explanation in a book published in 1499, sounds like a draft for a gravestone or memorial slab. There is no such memorial, but something much grander – the greatest memorial of all, the work of the books, which was already starting to change the world.

CHAPTER 9

Pressing to the Limits

𝕴t did not take Fust and Schöffer long to recover from catastrophe. They made a good team, until Fust's death in Paris. After that, Schöffer reaped where Gutenberg had sown, supplying missals across Central Europe – good business, no risk, high quality – for another forty years. He died, rich, respected and eminent, in 1503.

His career thus spanned the years in which Gutenberg's invention turned from a local wonder to an international phenomenon. Later, in the seventeenth century, when people began to ask how the revolution had happened, historians adopted a charming Latin name for these early printed books: they were the *incunabula* – the 'swaddling clothes', which by extension also means 'infancy' – of the printing revolution. This expression has now been taken into most major languages, sometimes acquiring a spurious singular form, *incunabulum*, sometimes a local equivalent: the German '*Wiegendruck*' means 'cradle-press' and the Japanese '*yoran-ki-bon*' means 'cradle-period books' (though they also use '*in-kyu-na-bu-ra*').

At about the same time as *incunabula* came into use, Johann Saubert of Nuremberg drew up the first catalogue of early books and imposed an arbitrary cutoff point of 1500. The term and the date fell neatly together. *Incunabula* are those books printed up to 31 December 1500. Other catalogues followed, of other collections; academics and collectors came on board; and today major universities and libraries around the world have their incunabulists. It's an academic industry. With the coming of computers, it became possible at last to pin down the whole subject, like some sort of literary human genome project, by listing everything published in movable type from Gutenberg's first *Donatus* up to 1500, wherever the volumes had ended up. The project, coordinated by London's British Library, is known as the Incunabula Short-Title Catalogue (ISTC). From its ninety-six contributing libraries in sixteen countries, the catalogue currently lists 28,360 titles, and rising, in virtually every European language (3,000 of them are on microfiche). By 1500 Europe's presses had printed some 15–20 million books.

I'm searching for an analogy. It has been called a media explosion, and it *was* in a way, when you consider how Mainz exploded in 1462, but an explosion dies as it expands. This grew, more like an animal population colonising new land. It was an entirely natural, spontaneous

expansion, flowing along trade routes, seeking out the likeli-
est nesting-sites — those towns with universities, cathedrals,
generous rulers, large law courts.

It was not entirely unrestrained. For ten years Schöffer
tried to preserve his monopoly by making his trainees
promise not to tell their secrets. There is a story that when
Johann Fust took samples of the *42-Line Bible* to sell in
Paris — Europe's biggest university, the Sorbonne, with
10,000 students: surely a terrific market — the guildsmen of
the book trade took one look and had this new rival chased
out of town for consorting with the devil. Scribal practices
endured, their products in demand for another twenty years.
And printed book prices, as with any new technology, did
not at once undercut manuscripts.

But the secret was out, and the market was hungry, and
prices dropped, and the boom was on.

For academics, this is well-trodden ground, the stuff of
detailed studies and theses. Rather than plod in the
footsteps of experts, I prefer to scan the territory, then
buttonhole you with some of the stories and connections
that strike me as particularly intriguing, those books that
seemed to do something new and — like Gutenberg's own
invention — inject into Europe elements which remain part
of life today.

❖ ❖ ❖

Germany proved an ideal base for expansion. It had good mines for the metals printers needed, good metalworkers, prosperous merchants with money to invest. For decades, Germans dominated the new trade, journeying with their sets of punch-cutting tools and hand moulds and formes, seeking financial backing and work wherever they could, settling for anything from a few weeks to years (Appendix II). Wherever these nomads went, they taught their trade to apprentices, who spread it further. Gutenberg's protégés from Strasbourg days, Heinrich Eggestein and Johann Mentelin, started works in their own home town and were in production as rivals by 1460, both printing their own versions of the first German translation of the Bible, which was the first Bible translation in any modern spoken language. It was a hopeless translation, but still a challenge to the traditional role of churchmen as interpreters of God's word. The archbishop of Mainz banned it in 1485 – one of the first acknowledgements that this new invention had the power to undermine establishments.

Apprentices from both Mainz offices scattered after the war of 1462, founding print shops in Cologne (1465–6), Basel (which issued its first Bible in 1468), Augsburg (1468) and Nuremberg (1470). Then, at an average rate of about eight new printers a year, printing spread to sixty German cities by 1500, many with two or more – Strasbourg had fifty by 1500 – making some 300 German printing works in all. Mainz itself, with half a dozen print shops, no longer figured high on the list, though Schöffer's sons, Johann and Peter, kept on the business after their father's death in 1502. Peter, a talented punch-cutter, worked in Worms, among other places, at a crucial historical moment we shall come to later.

Despite the scattering of the industry, one element – sales – remained centred if not on Mainz then at least nearby. Frankfurt, on the river route in the middle of Europe, had had a trade fair since the twelfth century, drawing traders from all Germany every spring and autumn. It was this fair that in the early fifteenth century gave Frankfurt its economic pre-eminence, while Mainz sank under the weight of its debt and destructive disputes. That was why Fust went there to hawk the *42-Line Bible* in October 1454. He or Schöffer or their salesman no doubt returned there every year, especially after books became a formal part of the fair in 1480. Today's Frankfurt Book Fair, with its hundreds of stands and tens of thousands of titles, is that fair's direct descendant.

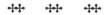

The most successful of all German printers arose in Nuremberg. This Bavarian town of some 50,000 people was one of Europe's richest and most advanced. Its double walls and 128 watchtowers assured safety for the trade that brought in the wealth. It made Mainz look like a backwater: paved streets, stone bridges across the Pegnitz, and water mains. Politically, it was not exactly progressive. Its thirty-five aristocratic families dominated the city council, which stood no nonsense from any guilds. But the system worked a dream. It was a city bound by success, a camaraderie displayed every Shrovetide in a famous carnival, at which masked townsfolk capered wildly through the city and staged dreadfully xenophobic plays, as if marking their walled den to keep Jews and Turks in their place. But xenophobia lived happily with its opposite. Merchants and their agents secured trading privileges in seventy cities. Nuremberg-owned companies monopolised refineries in Poland and Bohemia, and in light industry – arms, armour, brasswork – Nuremberg was supreme. As a result, its craftsmen were well off enough to have their own houses, which then as now was a good way to ensure against social unrest in the future. In Venice, six of the fifty-six rooms in Venice's ghetto for northerners, the Fondaco dei Tedeschi, were occupied by Nurembergers. So despite the lack of a university, the city was ambitious to be part of the intellectual mainstream flowing from Italy. It was, in brief, a natural home for the most astonishing of German *incunabula*: the first great attempt at popularisation, and the first book whose publication details are known, the *Nuremberg Chronicle*.

Hartmann Schedel graduated in medicine from Padua and practised as a doctor all his long life. But his real passion was books. He inherited several hundred from a cousin and spent his spare time and money collecting, creating an immense library which is now in the Bavarian State Library. He started to collect printed books in 1470, though he never abandoned script, copying forty volumes himself. A meticulous scholar and obsessive note-taker, he was a creative force only as a collector (his wife would take issue with me: he also fathered twelve children). Yet his peculiar obsessions drove him to write one of the most famous books of his day.

The fame of the *Nuremberg Chronicle* does not rest on originality. It purports to be a world history, in 600 pages, from the Creation to 1493. In fact it is a ragbag of information grabbed indiscriminately from hundreds of sources, predominantly Italian, notably our prolific friend Piccolomini, who besides being Pope, friend of Nicholas of Cusa and admirer of Gutenberg's Bible was no mean historian. Schedel had Piccolomini's *Historia Bohemica* (published in 1475, long after his death) and a manuscript of his history of Europe, and simply copied from them both. He was quite indiscriminate in what he included, ignoring vital contemporary events, like Columbus's discovery of America (news of which arrived just in time for inclusion). No: what marked it out was its illustrations, its design and its printing, which give it a unique place in the history of books.

The driving forces behind its publication were its patrons, Sebald Schreyer and Sebastian Kammermaister, both connoisseurs of Italian humanism and (crucially) woodcuts. It was their generous Renaissance ideals, to make the work available 'for the common delight', that underpinned the decision to publish in two parallel editions, Latin and German. Artists were to hand – Wilhelm Pleydenwurff, who had taught Albrecht Dürer, and one of his protégés, Michael Wohlgemut. Nuremberg was also home to Anton Koberger, godfather to Dürer, and Europe's biggest media tycoon; printer, publisher and bookseller all in one, he had two dozen presses, a hundred pressmen and agents all over Europe. Under his auspices, prices dropped and print runs rose from a mere 200 or so to over 1,000. He prefigured later publishers in social ambition: he married an aristocrat and cultivated the upper echelons, a publishing lord in all but name. Author, sources, patrons, artist, printer and distributor: the shared skills were all present in a unique, tight-knit group of well-off neighbours, friends and relatives.

Except for the print run, details of the *Chronicle's* production and contracts survive, presenting an extraordinary insight into this first work of popularisation. To run off an estimated 2,500 copies (1,500 in Latin, 1,000 in German), Koberger was required to provide a locked room for the workers to ensure there could be no plagiarism (it was pirated anyway after publication).* He bought the paper himself, invoicing his patrons later. He was paid four gulden for 500 pages: about £1/$1.50 per page, not far off the cost of printing and binding a present-day coffee-table book, if anyone did one in black and white.

It had over 1,800 illustrations, many, notoriously, being used twice or more. This gives an insight into the pressures, much the same then as now. The artists were working fourteen hours a day for their advance of 1,000 gulden − £100,000/$150,000, not bad, until you divide it by two and spread it over two years of production. And as time was of the essence, and not many people knew what Mantua and Verona really looked like, did they, so what the hell, why not just use the same view? Who cared, as long as they bought the book?

Well, they did and they didn't. In 1509 558 copies remained unsold. The artists' heirs, theoretically bound by contract to share the costs, found themselves charged with 1,200 gulden to cover unsold copies, returns and various other debts. This was more than their original advance;

* The first attempt to establish copyright came a few years later, in 1519, when a Jewish doctor, Paul Rici, in a translation of a medical treatise by the Muslim surgeon Abul Kasim (Albucasis), threatened excommunication to anyone pirating the work within six years of publication. It took another 200 years for copyright to be first protected legally (England, 1709).

there is no record, publishers will not be surprised to hear, of the advance being repaid. As Adrian Wilson says in *The Making of the Nuremberg Chronicle*: 'One can only conclude that the book trade has changed little in the intervening centuries and that the illustrator's lot was no better than it is today.'

The author, it should be noted, gets no mention at all. No contract, no advance, no royalties, nothing. Obviously no agent. It seems Schedel was just *thrilled* to be published, and did it for love. I would say this project lacked something in terms of editorial control. Its presiding genii, obsessed with design, production and sales, forgot about content and ended up with unsold copies and no profit.

There are obvious morals here. Overambitious publishers; uncritical patrons; no editorial control; probably the wrong author in the first place – the thing was heading for the rocks from the start. But then, like so many misplaced ventures, if hindsight had been foresight, we would not now have a wonderful book that is the very stuff of medieval life.

❖❖   ❖❖   ❖❖

Abroad, Germans spread under the same stimuli as at home, seeking markets among academics, prelates and lawyers. Germans trained more Germans and growth was exponential, until there were some 400 working all over Europe; and those are only the known ones. Appendix II lists those Germans who first went to the place mentioned. But many travelled on elsewhere, and so did their local trainees.

To list who went where and when would be fine work for a train-spotter: not a bad analogy, as it happens, because the interconnections become as intricate as a railway net-work, as hundreds and then thousands of printers estab-lished themselves and moved and returned across the face of Europe. Assuming it took three years to train a printer to a level at which he would be game to take off on his own, and suppose each master printer trained just one other (later, apprenticeships varied from two to five years), the expansion of expertise would have been exponential on a three-year base. Two master printers in 1452 produce only eight by 1460, but then 128 by 1470; 1,000 by 1480; 8,000 by 1490; 64,000 by 1500 . . . Well, by then competition had imposed Darwinian restraints, and the graph had levelled off. By 1500 some 1,000 printing works may have been employing 10–20,000 people.

Another way of looking at this expansion is to count up towns with presses. By 1480 – just twelve years after Guten-berg's death – 122 towns in Western Europe had printing presses, with or without German involvement. Almost half of them were in Italy.

Printing towns in Europe 1480

Italy:	50	Belgium:	5
Germany:	30	Switzerland:	5
France:	9	England:	4
Holland:	8	Bohemia:	2
Spain:	8		

Over the next twenty years the number of printing towns doubled again: 236 towns had one or more presses in 1500 (including, strangely, the village of Cetinje in Montenegro, where in 1493 the first Slavic press was set up, using Cyrillic type brought from Venice. It didn't last long; the Montenegrins melted down the lead for bullets).

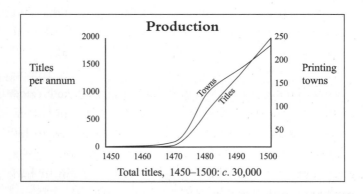

Production

Titles per annum

Printing towns

Total titles, 1450–1500: *c.* 30,000

✢✢   ✢✢   ✢✢

Italy owes a particular debt to young Konrad Sweynheym —
from Schwanheim, between Mainz and Frankfurt — who
was possibly a Gutenberg protégé and may well have benefited from the (always theoretical) link between Gutenberg
and Nicholas of Cusa.

In 1459 Nicholas, bishop of Brixen in the Tyrol, had
been having a hard time with the local Austrian ruler. His
old friend Piccolomini, now Pope Pius II, had invited him
to Rome. 'Such abilities as yours,' he wrote, 'should not be
allowed to languish imprisoned among snows and gloomy
defiles.' In Rome, Nicholas, who had done so much to
reform Germany's corrupt monasteries, became incensed at
what he saw. 'Everything is corrupt! No one does his job
properly! Neither you nor the cardinals take the interests of
the Church truly to heart!' (This is Pius himself reporting
the conversation, by the way, in a remarkably frank and
vivid piece of self-criticism. He was, as I said, a writer at
heart.) In reply, Pius told Nicholas to take a break.

Subiaco, seventy kilometres east of Rome, was a good
place for a retreat, charmingly set in hills, by a lake created
for the emperor Nero. St Benedict had turned hermit here in
a cave, inspiring a Benedictine monastery dedicated to his
twin sister, St Scholastica. And Nicholas, remember, was a
great supporter of the Benedictines, through whom he had
worked for reform in Germany.

Was it just another of those coincidences that it was to

Subiaco – in particular to the Santa Scholastica monastery – that young Sweynheym and his friend Johann Pannartz came when they headed south in 1464? Not a coincidence at all, according to the preface of the Sweynheym–Pannartz edition of St Jerome, published in 1470. The preface was written by Giovanni Andrea de Bussi, who had been secretary to Nicholas of Cusa and was now chief librarian to the Vatican. So he, like his former boss, had an interest in arguing that printing, about which the Pope might still have his doubts, was a divine blessing, 'a gift of happiness for the Christian world'. He went on:

> It is perhaps no slight glory for Your Holiness that volumes which in former times could scarce be bought for a hundred gold pieces are today to be had for reading in good versions and free of faults throughout for twenty . . . One can hardly report inventions of like importance for mankind, whether in ancient or modern times.

And then comes this telling sentence: 'It is that which the soul (rich in honours and meriting heaven) of Nicholas of Cusa . . . so fervently desired: that this holy art, whose shoots became visible at that time in Germany, should be transplanted to Roman soil.'

There is, of course, no evidence for a link, but it is easy to imagine one: Nicholas in Subiaco, with book-loving

Benedictines whose colleagues in Mainz were close to the events that swirled around the invention of printing, and were central to the dispute over the rival archbishops (this is 1459, when Mainz's civil war began to brew). By now he would have known about the *42-Line Bible*. Maybe his own copy, the one that's now in Vienna, had already reached Brixen, and he would soon be ordering his copy of the *Catholicon* (it's still in his library at the Cusanus Research Centre in Bernkastel-Kues). Imagine a letter to his old friend, Gutenberg, mentioning how ideal Subiaco would be: the monastery, the Benedictines, the judicious distance from Rome and its dubious Pope. If ever any German printer wanted to come south, this would be a good place to start.

Letter or no, Sweynheym and Pannartz made it to Subiaco in 1464 – there the next year to produce Italy's first printed book, the works of an obscure early Christian convert, Firmianus Lactantius – and on to Rome, printing twenty-eight titles in all. Then things went wrong. Over-production in Italy was the problem. Their market dried up, and their house filled with unsold, unbound books. In 1472 Bussi put in a word for them with the Pope, but to no avail. Pannartz died soon afterwards, and Sweynheym turned to map-engraving.

These two were just the first of many to heed the call. Ulrich Hahn, a possible Bamberg trainee, was in Rome in

1466. Hans (or Johann) von Speyer and his brother Wende-
lin, both Mainz-trained, were granted a monopoly in Venice
in 1467, as his Latin colophon proudly proclaimed: 'The
first to print books by means of bronze formes in the
Adriatic city was Johann, who originated in Speyer.' There
the von Speyer brothers were joined by Nicholas Jenson, the
French spy sent to learn what he could from Gutenberg,
now a spy no more, because he had stayed on in Germany as
a master punch-cutter before heading south. Jenson devised
the superb Roman typeface which was used to print the first
Bible in Italian, in 1471, thus marking a break with Germany's script-based, hard-to-read textura. After Johann's death,
his monopoly lapsed, and Jenson set up on his own. Johann
Numeister, another Gutenberg protégé, settled in Foligno
and produced the first edition of Dante's *Divine Comedy* in
1472. (Incidentally, this was now a two-way process:
Numeister trained Stephen Arndes from Hamburg, who
returned to Germany and set up a major works in Lübeck
in 1486.) A German-Jewish family, naming themselves
Soncino after their first home town in Italy, became the first
to publish in Hebrew; the founder's nephew, Gerson ben
Moses, was known as Menzlein, the Little Mainzer, in
memory of the origins of his skill. By 1480 Italy far outdid
Germany in the number of printing centres.

And Venice was printing capital not simply of Italy but of all Europe, with 150 presses. Success came for many reasons. It was a city-state that had preserved its independence from the dynastic rivalries of its neighbours. It was beautifully positioned for land and sea commerce, which it exploited to make itself Europe's richest city. And it had within reach of its ships the Greek-speaking world of Byzantium. Thus, when the Turks seized Constantinople in 1453 and turned it into Istanbul, it was to Venice that its scholars fled, forming a community of expatriate academics, *La scuola e la nazione greca*, and creating an irony. The Fall of Constantinople was a notorious disaster for Christendom; yet it contributed to a boom in scholarship in Europe. The date 29 May 1453 was one of few implanted in my nine-year-old brain, because it was the birthday of the Renaissance, the date on which Europeans began to think and paint properly. As historical analysis, this lacks nuance; but it does emphasise that the law of unintended consequences, usually assumed to state that well-meant acts pave paths to hell, may also specify the opposite. It certainly did in this case. The influx of Greeks and their manuscripts fuelled a feeling among Renaissance scholars and artists that, in their search for classical anteced-ents, they had better explore their pre-Latin roots among the writings of the ancient Greeks.

One such scholar was a diffident provincial named Teobaldo Manucci, who in 1480 was teaching the young princes Alberto and Lionello Pio, of Carpi. Teobaldo, a graduate of Rome and Ferrara, got to know the boys' uncle, Prince Giovanni Pico of Mirandola. Pico was both very rich and very brilliant, being fluent not only in Latin and Greek, but also Hebrew and Arabic — astonishing erudition for a man just out of his teens who died at the age of thirty-one. Through Pico, Teobaldo Manucci, now Latinised as Aldus Manutius, passed to Pico's friend and fellow scholar Ermolao Barbaro of Venice.

In Venice, already so rich in printers that competition had driven many out of business, Aldus spotted a gap in the market. Despite the boom in Greek studies, no one was publishing in Greek. The local Greeks didn't have the technology, and Greek handwriting had never been standardised. This struck the shy, Greek-speaking teacher as a terrible lack. How could classical literature underpin education, as it should, if there were no texts? Once stated, it was obvious. He found backers – his former pupils among them – devised a typeface, had punches cut and went into business. It was risky, of course, but the cost and originality enabled him to apply for and receive a twenty-year monopoly on the printing of Greek books. With this security, he published Aristotle, in five volumes (1495–8), going on to publish dozens of other major classical works, to the highest standards – he required his Greek typesetters and proof-correctors to speak classical Greek, or get fired. His commitment, his programme and his standards established the Aldine Press as Venice's leading printer, and a tradition of Greek printing that lasted until the end of the nineteenth century.

⊹⊹ ⊹⊹ ⊹⊹

All of which is by way of background to allow me to examine one of the craziest, most beautiful books ever printed.

The book has a lovely mouthful of a title: *Hypnerotomachia Poliphili*, which roughly translates as *Poliphilo's Struggle for Love in a Dream*. The title says much about the book. The two invented words, in a literal translation, mean 'sleepy-erotic-strife of many-loves'. It is an excessive, hothouse sort of a title.

So is the plot. In some ways it is a stock pastoral fantasy, with an enamoured hero pursuing, finding and accompanying his beloved Polia, aided and abetted by nymphs, through landscapes and numerous buildings. At the end, just as consummation seems inevitable, Polia vanishes into thin air.

But this plot unfolds in a lunatic fashion. Poliphilo falls asleep in a forest and dreams for much of the book. In his dream, at the request of nymphs, Polia tells her story, which proceeds until she meets Poliphilo and a priestess, who asks to hear Poliphilo's story, in which he tells of a pseudo-death, visions and an awakening in Polia's arms. Except that he's still dreaming, dreaming that Polia ends her narrative. That's when they embrace and she dissolves. He wakes. The end.

A baffling Russian-doll structure is just the start of the confusions. The book is written in an artificial language, which uses Italian grammar with words drawn from Latin, Tuscan and Greek, many of them totally made up, with Italian endings. There are also eighty epigrams and inscriptions, in Greek, Hebrew, Latin, mock hieroglyphs and 'Chaldean'. It is the work of a cryptomaniac. Astonishingly, *HP* has been translated into English, in part in 1592 (only a third of it), and in full in 1999 by an American academic, Joscelyn Godwin, Professor of Music at Colgate University, Hamilton, NY. Godwin had been in love with the book for years and completed his translation for the five hundredth anniversary of its publication, brilliantly adapting it to pull back from the extreme and deliberate obscurantism of the original. He gives an impression of what a sentence would be like if he had matched the author's classically based neologisms and style: 'In this horrid and cuspidinous littoral and most miserable site of the algent and fetorific lake stood saevious Tisiphone, efferal and cruel with her viparine capillament, her meschine and miserable soul, implacably furibund.'

Through the author's interconvolvulated coruscations, as he might have put it, palpitates an umbracious erotomania:

in other words, it throbs with repressed sexuality. Both the hero and heroine are wildly, triumphantly, assertively erotic. Here is a description of Botticellian nymphs at play, girls 'of tender years, redolent with the bloom of youth and beautiful beyond belief, together with their beardless lovers . . . They had gathered their thin silken dresses, bright with many attractive colours, and bundled them up in their snow-white arms, showing the elegant form of their solid thighs . . . They kissed with juicy and tremulous tongues nourished with fragrant musk, playfully penetrating each other's wet and laughing lips . . .' And so on, for many pages.

Weirdly, the book's erotic content is expressed most powerfully through buildings, which form a series of stages for the action. Indeed, buildings take up more than half the book, and no fewer than seventy-eight of the first eighty-six pages are descriptions of buildings or gardens. Of the 172 engravings, eighty-eight are of buildings. In sequence we are led through a garden planted to look like a wilderness, a palm grove, a giant pyramid (which takes up fifty pages), a bridge, octagonal baths, a palace, an arena, a gateway, a gymnasium, a colonnade, a courtyard, two colossi, a statue of an elephant carrying an obelisk, another bridge, a bath-house, a pergola and an aquatic labyrinth. The love story is a mere adjunct.

Yet story and buildings are interfused, in a quite extraor-

dinary way. Poliphilo is a 'lover of many things', and Polia
is a neuter plural – 'many things'. And it is in architectural
things that Poliphilo finds release for his pent-up passions, for
buildings are symbols of the body. I have never heard of
building fetishism, but here it is: this is nothing less than an
architectural erotic fantasy. An arch is virginal, marble as
flawless as a nymph's skin. Buildings fill Poliphilo with the
'highest carnal pleasure' and 'burning lust'. A temple of
Bacchus is carved with a 'rigidly rigorous' phallus. Pining
for Polia and questing for love, Poliphilo becomes enrap-
tured by what he sees, but is at first frustrated, as a female
statue bears the words 'Do not touch my body'. Later,
though, he enters a temple, which becomes a stage for ever
more explicit rites. Doors are opened wonderfully smoothly
by magnetic stones, inscribed in Latin and Greek with 'let
each follow his own pleasure'. A priestess sets a torch
aflame then inserts it into a cistern, asking a nymph what
her wish is. 'Holy Priestess,' she replies, 'I ask grace for him
[Poliphilo] that together we may attain the amorous king-
dom', while Poliphilo himself begs that 'Polia should keep
me no longer vacillating in such amorous torment'. The
nymph, 'with a sigh uttered hotly from the bottom of her
inflamed heart', admits that she is actually Polia and that
'your persistent love has altogether stolen me away from the
college of chastity, and forced me to extinguish my torch'.
To this Poliphilo 'inflamed from head to foot . . . dissolved

in sweet and amorous tears and lost myself completely'. At the end of these love rites he 'instantly felt the solid earth stir and shudder', and 'the groaning hinges of the golden doors sounded beneath the vaults like a thunderclap trapped in a sinuous cavern'. The very building, it seems, shares in Poliphilo's orgasm. Some of the illustrations would even now rate as soft-core pornography (many of the offending organs being inked out in the Vatican's copy). In the end, this is the story of Poliphilo's progress from lover to lover, sex object to sex object. The phrase '*amor vincit omnia*' ('love conquers all') echoes in many illustrations; 'Eros is the mother of everything' is carved into a mountain in Latin, Greek and Hebrew. How different, how very refreshingly different, from the abhorrence felt by pre-Renaissance churchmen – just compare this with the dreadful flagellants of Northern Europe of recent memory – towards both buildings and the human body.

What sort of person would write such stuff? And how on earth did it get printed? The book was ostensibly anonymous, which is why I have not mentioned the author's name so far. However, the decorated capitals at the start of its thirty-eight chapters spell out a sentence – POLIAM FRATER FRANCISCVS COLVMNA PERAMAVIT ('Brother Francesco Colonna greatly loved Polia'). Since '*polia*' means 'many things', this sounds like a secret confession of his eclectic sexual tastes. This Colonna has long been assumed to be one who lived in the monastery of Saints John and Paul in Venice, notorious for being 'unreformed' and therefore rather lax in its standards, which meant that its monks were allowed to live outside the monastery and do pretty much what they liked. Until his death at the age of ninety-four, scandalous to the end, what Colonna liked, it seems, was women, architecture and gardens, which became the means for an encyclopedic exploration of 'all that could be known', all knitted into a surreal narrative. He was able to indulge these passions thanks to the astonishing generosity, or gullibility, of his patron, Leonardo Grassi or Crasso, who paid Aldus Manutius to produce the book.

The result, in commercial terms, was a disaster. It seems to have been suicidal to start with, for in an introduction the patron wrote that the author 'devised his work so that only the wise may penetrate the sanctuary . . . These things are not for the populace.' How right he was. Hardly anyone bought it (though Aldus himself must have been proud of his achievement, for he adopted one illustration of a dolphin and an anchor as the famous Aldine Press emblem, symbol-ising activity tempered by restraint).

A commercial failure; but in terms of looks and sub-sequent reputation, *HP* became a wonder. Within half a century it was a cult book, especially in France. Its typeface, deriving from Jenson's Roman, evokes the typographic equivalent of lust. One print historian, George Painter, described it as 'tall in uprights and firmly seriphed, both bold and delicate, equally dark and radiant in its blacks and whites'. (Resurrected and named *Poliphilus*, it was to have been used in a 1920s translation that was never made, finally emerging in Joscelyn Godwin's new translation; and in the words you are now reading: this book is set in Poliphilus.) *HP* has those gorgeous decorated initials, and numerous Roman-style inscriptions, triumphantly proclaiming the perfection of classical standards that may still be glimpsed among the ruins of the past, and asserting the dominance of Roman lettering over Gutenberg-style Gothic. The illustrations have suggested to different art historians the influence, if not direct involvement, of a range of brilliant artists – Mantegna, Giocondo, Bellini, Botticelli and/or Raphael. The design is a masterpiece, with text, illustrations, captions and epigrams beautifully combined. The text is often shaped to fit underneath or round its picture, and it is occasionally set in the shape of a goblet. Nothing quite like it appeared until the avant-garde books of the early twentieth century, and collectors would die – or at least pay up to £500,000/ $750,000 – for any of its surviving hundred or so copies. To some it is quite simply the most beautiful non-religious book ever printed.

Its reputation is also based on a completely different judgement, which ignores its language and design and sees it entirely as a visual treatise on classical architecture, covering a wide range of buildings, with all the related terminology. Every building mentioned has its ancient sources, here a temple related to the Mausoleum of Helicarnassus, there a paving deriving from the mosaics of Palestrina. But these are not just real buildings: the book explores imaginary ones, virtual ones, dream ones a mile high, or lit through impossibly narrow slits, or as transparent as the Crystal Palace.

So total is the expertise that one expert, Liane Lefaivre, of the Technical University, Delft, has written a book devoted to the proposition that the author was not Colonna at all, but the greatest and most polymathic of Renaissance architects, Leon Battista Alberti, who used similar sources and similar stylistic habits. She makes a strong case (though not one that has been widely accepted), linking Alberti with another Francesco Colonna altogether, a Roman, not a Venetian. So perhaps the acrostic is not a signature, but a discreet dedication.

Hypnerotomachia would surely have astonished Gutenberg. Nothing could be a more logical or surprising consequence of his Bible than this extravagant, pagan, totally uncommercial venture, nothing so foreign to his own austere, commercial and religious intentions.

In France and England, where printing was as significant as

everywhere else, the trade developed without such a close dependence on German enterprise, and also without the hectic competition. It's as if the cultures are infused with a rising tide rather than battered and swept by a *tsunami*.

In Paris, intellectual life was dominated by the Sorbonne. Here, twenty-four stationers, selling their wares through four booksellers, were contracted by the university to copy traditional academic texts. But during the fifteenth century teachers – led by Guillaume Fichet – also wanted access to the Greek and Roman writers who were behind the growth of humanism in Italy. In 1470 the rector of the Sorbonne happened to be a German, Johann Heynlin. The two of them imposed a different printing ethos in Paris. With Fichet's backing, Heynlin invited two of his countrymen, Ulrich Gering from Constance and Michael Friburger from Colmar, to set up a print shop, and told them what to print. This was the first time that publishing emerged as a separate operation from printing – the beginning of spec-ialisations that would, in the end, lead to numerous dedi-cated activities: publishing, typefounding, composing, printing, binding, selling.

William Caxton, England's first printer, would be of significance for the sole reason that he *wasn't a German*. This is not a theme to set the world aflame. But the fact is that Caxton was well established as a diplomat and businessman before he became a printer, and in his new profession he was able to stand on the shoulders of his predecessors. It is not his technical competence that marks him out. It is his commitment to publishing in English, thus starting the long process of reducing a chaos of inflections and dialects to a simpler, common tongue.

Caxton was a cloth-merchant, who in 1462, in his early forties, found himself looking after British trading interests in Bruges, ruling his little colony as both an ambassador and a governor. A few years before his governorship ended in 1470, he started work on a translation of a collection of legends about Troy, compiled by a French priest and dedi-cated to the Duke of Burgundy. Pretty soon he gave it up, perhaps because he saw no chance of selling it in an England in the midst of the civil war that came to be called the Wars of the Roses. But then, when his governorship ended, he was summoned to the Burgundian court. It so happened that the current duchess was Margaret of York, sister of King Edward IV. She had been married to Charles the Bold of Burgundy two years before, when Charles was trying to establish Burgundy as an independent country, and needed England as an ally against the French. The glorious marriage celebrations were still the talk of the country. In his audience, she asked to see his translations, offered a correc-tion or two, and commissioned him to complete it. He then moved to Cologne, where he set to work. It was almost too much for him. His pen became worn – as he wrote – his hand weary, and his eye dimmed with the effort.

It was in Cologne that he heard of a better way to reproduce script. Ulrich Zel, one of Peter Schöffer's protégés, had set up shop there in 1466, and one of *his* assistants was Johann Veldener, whom Caxton contracted 'at his great charge and dispense' either as a teacher or a printer of his book, or both. This was quite a risk, justified presumably by his ambition to exploit a new market, the production of books in English. Having learned his business and bought a press and type, he acquired a faithful assistant, Wynkyn de Worde, a German from Wörth, 100 kilometres south of Mainz (there's no escaping the German connection quite yet). Gambling his capital on buying paper, he produced the first printed book in English, the 700-page *Recuyell* ('*recueil*': 'summary') *of the historyes of Troye*, probably in late 1471, probably in Cologne, though possibly a year or two later in Bruges, where he re-established his business.

In 1476 he was back in London, in the precincts of Westminster Abbey, with England's first printing press. Modesty was becoming his salient trait, for he had come to this business late in life and always gave the charming impression that he felt lucky that it was the 'symple person William Caxton' to whom the responsibility of printing in English had fallen. His success was rooted in self-doubt. He knew French well enough to recognise his imperfections, and he was not at all sure about his own language. How high-falutin should he be, how simple, how direct, how local in his expression? 'Pardonne me of this rude and comyn Englyshe, where as shall be found faulte,' he wrote in a dedication to the Queen Mother, Lady Margaret Beaufort, 'for I confess me not learned ne knowing the art of rethoryk ne of such gaye termes as now be said in these dayes.' He need not have worried. He aimed as he said to produce an 'englyshe not over rude ne curyous', and succeeded wonderfully, producing 100 books which together, in the words of one biographer, Lotte Hellinga, form 'a monument to one man's delight in sharing with others his respect for texts (to which he gave new form) and his pleasure in reading them'.

His success, which made him rich, also laid the foundations of two factors that are with us still: the linguistic dominance of London and the many illogicalities that so baffle foreigners. English was undergoing extraordinarily rapid change at the time, as Caxton himself noted: 'Certaynly our langage now used varyeth ferre [far] from that which was used and spoken when I was borne.' Chaucer, born the previous century, is much harder to understand than Caxton's English, as Caxton himself revealed: he caught Chaucer's old-fashioned complexity in his most famous publication, *The Canterbury Tales* of 1477, upgraded in 1483. Old forms – adjectival inflections, odd plurals (like *eyren* for *eggs*), variable past tenses (*ached/oke, climbed/clomb*) – were on the way out, as Bill Bryson notes in *Mother Tongue*. If you travelled eighty kilometres out of London, there was no certainty you would be understood. In London they prayed 'Forgive us our trespasses', but in Kent they prayed 'And vorlet ous oure yeldinges'. It fell to Caxton to pickle in type variant forms which might well have vanished: *half/halves, grass/graze, bath/bathe*, and even a triplet or two: *life/lives*, the second of which has two forms, long and short, as in 'a cat with nine lives lives next door'. It's tough luck on anyone learning English today that Caxton happened along just when people still wrote *knight* in the way Chaucer had pronounced it, something like *ker-n-ich-t*, more like its Germanic root, *Knecht*, than the *nite* of Caxton's day, and our own.

All of this is of immense significance for the evolution of English. For the history of printing, however, Caxton's story is one of effects rather than causes. By the time of his death in 1491, the heady days of research and development were over, and all Europe was busy with the consequences.

Postscript

Yet at Europe's southern fringes the inexorable advance of the printing press proved suddenly and surprisingly exor-able. It stopped dead in its tracks, blocked by the world of Islam.

Now this, to European eyes, is something of a mystery. Islam, having established itself by the sword, had then developed an entirely different dimension, in which scholarship, art and science thrived. By 1000 it was as a cultural, religious and trading unity that Islam dominated the world beyond Europe's frontiers, from Spain to the Punjab. One trader had a warehouse on the Volga and another in Gujarat. Arab dinars were used in Finland, and Arab slavetraders in the central Sahara could write cheques honoured in Cairo. This was not a world of inwardlooking extremists. Hungry for learning, Islamic scholars looked back to the Greeks for their foundations in science and philosophy, and translated Greek classics *en masse*. Books were loved, honoured and collected into vast libraries: Cairo's had 200,000 books, Bukhara's had 45,000. In the eleventh century Avicenna (ibn Sina, as he was in Arabic) was known as the 'Aristotle of the East'; his medical encyclopedia was Europe's preeminent medical textbook for 300 years (as a tribute to the international nature of fifteenthcentury scholarship, it was printed in a Hebrew translation by the GermanJewish printer, Josef ben Jakob Gunzenhauser Ashkenazi – 'the German from Gunzenhausen' – in Naples). It was the Arabs who seized on the Indian numerical system we now term Arabic. Their science gave Europeans countless terms – alchemy (*'alkimiya'*, 'transformation'), zero (*'sifr'*, 'empty'), algebra (*'aljabr'*, 'reunion'). Baghdad vastly exceeded Rome in wealth even if you discount the hyperbole of many

Muslim accounts. In the tenth century one caliph greeted a Byzantine ruler with 160,000 cavalrymen and 100 lions, conducting his awed guest to a palace decorated with 38,000 curtains and 22,000 rugs.

With its wealth, scholastic traditions and urban comforts, Islam, you might think, was a perfect seedbed for the printing press. The Muslims had paper; they had ink; they even had wine presses, for the stern injunction against all alcohol came later. Moreover, Arabic is an alphabetical script. The fact that letters have four different forms, depending on their position, offers no great problem to punch-cutters and typesetters – after all, Gutenberg coped with up to a dozen different forms of the same letter.

Yet what happened when confronted with the possibilities inherent in Gutenberg's invention?

Absolutely nothing.

Print made no impact at all on the Muslim world for 400 years, until the nineteenth century, when Muslims in India started printing tracts, and then newspapers. By the beginning of the twentieth century, Muslims in India's north-west provinces and the Punjab were publishing 4–5,000 books every decade.

So why the gap?

It was not through lack of awareness, for knowledge of printing came with Jewish refugees fleeing from persecution in Spain to Constantinople. For much of the fifteenth

century the million Jews in Spain – in the throes of libera-
tion from Arabs, or 'Moorish' rule – were well established,
with government positions and fine academics. But their
advance often depended on conversion to Christianity to
avoid Christian anti-Semitism. In 1492, with the final defeat
of the Moors, the Inquisition came into its own, and offered
the Jews a choice: convert or get out. Some 20,000 families,
perhaps 100,000 people, chose exile, taking with them their
skills, among which was printing. In 1493 Jewish refugees in
Constantinople produced the first books in Hebrew. A
Qur'an was printed in Arabic in Italy by 1500. A generation
later, in 1530, Gershom ben Moses, the grandson of Israel
Nathan Soncino, founder of the great Jewish-German-
Italian publishing family, set up in Istanbul, and later moved
to Cairo. There is no way that an educated Muslim could
not have known about printing or its potential.

And yet from Muslim traders, scholars, administrators,
not a flicker of interest, or outright hostility. When the first
printing works was established in Istanbul in 1729 by an
ex-slave who had gone into government service and con-
verted to Islam, he managed to print just seventeen titles
before religious opposition became so intense that the press
was closed down in 1742.

Again: why? To historians, it's something of a problem,
because no Muslim leader ever commented on the matter at
the time. As one scholar, Francis Robinson, Professor of

History at Royal Holloway, University of London, says, 'current scholarship is unsure why Muslims rejected printing for so long'. Some superficial reasons come to mind but fail to persuade. Perhaps it was because scribal traditions were embedded in Islam, or because calligraphy was and is revered as the highest of Islamic arts? But such traditions were strong in fifteenth-century Europe as well. Perhaps because there would have been opposition to innovation, especially non-Islamic innovation? There is something in this, for Europe was now in the throes of worldwide explo-ration that bypassed the Islamic world, and reinforced its defensive, inward-looking conservatism; but still practical advances, from the flintlock to the electric light, eventually found acceptance.

As Robinson says, and as any Muslim will confirm, the answer lies in some fundamental Islamic assumptions about the nature of truth. For Muslims, the Qur'an is the word of God, even more so than the Bible is for Christians or the Torah for Jews. The Qur'an's beauty is a proof of God's existence. And 'Qur'an' means 'recitation'. Its divinity is realised by being learned and read aloud. Its words are, as Constance Padwick puts it in *Muslim Devotions*, 'the twigs of the burning bush aflame with God'. It was written only as an aid to memory and oral transmission. The Egyptian standard edition of the Qur'an printed in the 1920s was produced not from a study of variant manuscripts but from fourteen different *recitations*. To be a *Hafidh*, someone who can recite the whole thing from memory, was and is a high honour.

And this infused all other instruction. An author's work acquired authority only when read back to the author by a scribe. In a Quranic school (*madrasa*) the teacher would dictate and the pupils write, but the purpose was always to transfer an oral text from memory to memory. The book was secondary. In the words of an Islamic verse, 'Books die, but memory lives'. Indeed, the proof of 'lawfulness' was provided by an *ijaza*, a list of those who had transmitted the content of a work orally, from person to person. Thus 'the pupil was the trustee in his generation of part of the great tradition of Islamic learning handed down from the past'.

Finally, it was, of course, in the interests of the religious rulers to emphasise this, as was the way of priestly elites in ancient Egypt and Mesopotamia. Imams would not willingly have done themselves out of a job by allowing people direct access to knowledge. This would have been to open the way to *bida* (innovation), a virtual heresy. True, Islam adopted print in nineteenth-century British India, but only because they were losing out to Christian missionaries and Hinduism. In Robinson's words, 'print changed from being a threat to their authority to the means by which they might prop it up, indeed promote it'. In Catholicism, print was initially seen as a divine gift, only later assuming devilish traits; in Islam it was devilish for 400 years, until a greater evil cast it as a lesser one.

What is revealed in the Islamic response to printing is part of a continuing and widespread distrust of the written word in conservative societies. As Barbara Metcalf, Professor of History at the University of California, Davis, writes, Hindu Vedic traditions were rooted in the notion that 'truth is tied to the living words of authentic persons'. This attitude goes back to ancient Greece, which was also wedded to the oral transmission of knowledge. When the alphabet – 'Phoenician writing', as the Greeks called it – made its breakthrough into Greek culture, in around 750 BC, it filtered in from below, being adopted by artisans in contact with Phoenician traders. Two hundred and fifty years later, many intellectuals were still not sure that writing was a good idea. 'If men learn this,' wrote Plato, 'it will plant forgetfulness in their souls.' For true wisdom, you need human interaction, with good teachers. Once their words are in a book, the whole process breaks down.

For Muslims, as Robinson says, printing 'attacked what was understood to make knowledge trustworthy, what gave it value and authority'. No more authorised transmission, no more memory, all authority gone, and God's will undermined.

No wonder Gutenberg's invention came up against a brick wall.

CHAPTER 10

Christendom Divided, the World United

From Mainz, the printing press conquered Europe, and from Europe the world. Its effects became part of all of us, with the odd consequence that the details have not been much analysed. In the words of someone who has written the best review of the subject, Elizabeth Eisenstein, 'those who seem to agree that momentous changes were entailed always seem to stop short of telling us just what they were'. Luckily, I can stop short as well, because this is a book about beginnings. What follows is a flavour of the new universe opened by Gutenberg, and a sharp focus on the second explosion set off by his invention.

❖❖   ❖❖   ❖❖

Scribes were gone. An Italian businessman, Vespaniano da Bisticci, employed forty-five scribes to produce 200 books for Cosimo de Medici's library in the 1460s and pretended to despise the new invention, but by 1478 he was out of business. Scribes actually copied printed typefaces – now evolving away from their scribal roots – in a vain attempt to hold back the flood, to no avail. Along with the scribes went the illuminators and their gorgeous work of decorating capitals and margins.

In their place came new specialities. Markets expanded, building on their own success, in a flurry of feedbacks. Accountancy books were bought by authors writing more accountancy books; books on etiquette ostensibly to teach demureness to young ladies sold to their anxious parents and tutors; shepherds did not buy shepherds' almanacs, but poets did (as, in our own time, country diaries of Edwardian ladies do not sell to gardeners, nor survival manuals to survivors, nor brief histories of the universe to astronomers, unless they all happen to be wondering how to write bestsellers).

Printing, of course, allowed the spread of reason, science and scholarship, but rather slowly. What sold fast was good old-fashioned dross: astrology, alchemy and esoteric lore (Gutenberg leading the way with his reproduction of *Sibylline Prophecies*). Cosimo de Medici gathered a mass of dialogues attributed to the Egyptian god Thoth, whose Greek name was Hermes Trismegistus. Books on so-called 'hermetic' lore formed a medieval equivalent of New Age publishing, catering to the belief that the past was a treasury of ancient wisdom. It fitted well with the secretive nature of those who had an interest in preserving an aura of secrecy, like guildsmen – and to some extent printers, who in some eyes acquired the status of divine or satanic adepts (witness the confusion in the Coster legend of Fust with the medieval necromancer Faust).

Still, reason, science and scholarship advanced. For the first time specialists could agree on their agendas and feed off each other, as if stabilised by the whirling gyroscope of printing. Once, the norms of classical architecture were known only from a few hand-copied manuscripts, or from personal observation, or from travelling experts. Now Vit-ruvius, who laid down the rules of classical architecture around the time of Christ, could be reproduced in all major languages, and architects armed with the works of Vitruvius's modern disciples – Giacomo Vignola and Andrea Palladio – could eventually re-create Greek and Roman glories in estates from Yorkshire to St Petersburg. When the map-maker Abraham Ortelius published a collection of maps in his *Theatrum orbis terrarum* in Ant-werp in 1570, it acted as a focus for new information, leading to an explosion of geographical knowledge that inspired twenty-eight editions by the time he died in 1598. Scientists gathering information from newly discovered lands – this was the century in which the New World was opened and the earth first circumnavigated – could stand

on each other's shoulders in recording distant plants, ani-
mals, landforms, cities and peoples. In Ortelius's early
editions, paradise had its place; later he admitted that he
didn't really know where it was ('By Paradise,' he said, 'I
do think the blessed life to be understood') and dropped it.

In this, the print shops of Europe became a force for
commercial and academic change. The master printer
emerged as a social force, coordinating finance, authors,
proofreaders, suppliers, punch-cutters, typefounders, pressmen and salesmen, rivalling each other with promises of
clearer title pages and better indexes and ever more perfect
proofreading. But the print shops were also mini-universities
under their deans, the master printers, attracting multi-
lingual scholars, gathering and dispersing information. (It
worked both ways: literati loved to mess with ink, compose a
page and use a press.) In Italy, the home from home of the
printing press, it found good rich earth already bursting with
the growths of Renaissance art and scholarship. It was the
printing press that seized these creative forces and catapulted
them across the face of Europe.

For the first time people began to form a more accurate
picture of their own past. In medieval scribal culture, it was
hard to know what was known, because nothing could be
checked without copying and selling manuscripts or visiting
every library. To advance, existing knowledge – if you can
call what is not widely known 'knowledge' – had to be

recovered. Hence the significance of the classical revival, which, once in full flow, quickly moved on from being a wellspring to a foundation for further progress. It remained widely believed that the earth was, in accordance with biblical and Jewish tradition, no more than about 6,000 years old. To upset that timescale would demand the opening of another ancient book, the pages of which are geological strata. But historical time fits into those six millennia, and it began to acquire substance as authors and translators piled up information about vanished civilisations from Pharaonic Egypt forward.

Print inspired new forms of writing. In the old days rulers had addressed followers, or lawyers had addressed courts, and their words endured, if at all, as records. Popular works of literature, as opposed to works of scholarship, record or instruction, were rarities (like Dante's *Divine Comedy*, Boccaccio's *Decameron*, or Chaucer's *Canterbury Tales*, or even Piccolomini's *Two Lovers*, a novel included in a letter). Now the possibility existed of addressing directly anyone, anywhere – in theory, *everyone* who could read – if only they could be reached and spoken to persuasively, in the vernacular as opposed to Latin. No one had ever done that before (at least, not in books). New styles would be invented. In a castle tower near Bordeaux, Montaigne would write what he called 'essays', telling you and me about himself. Somewhere in Spain an unknown writer would produce the first true novel of the new medium (*The Life of Lazarillo de Tormes*, 1554).

Science, particularly astronomy, was a little slow off the mark, because there was a lot of the past to absorb before new research produced new theories. But printing allowed a foundation for progress. Germany produced the greatest fifteenth-century astronomer in Johann Müller, born in Königsberg ('King's Mountain'), which he adopted in a Latinised form as his surname: Regiomontanus. He studied Ptolemy, whose *Almagest* explained planetary movements in terms of perfect circles moving around the earth; he learned Greek; realised the inadequacies of current astronomical records; and moved to Nuremberg at about the time Koberger was getting started. There he set up both an observatory and a printing press, to publish his detailed observations of the position of the moon and planets. In 1474 he came up with an entirely new method that offered the possibility of calculating longitude by working out the distance to the moon, a system that proved so complicated that no one could make it work. Though armed with one of Regiomontanus's almanacs, Columbus was none the wiser about his position when he stumbled on America twenty years later. Still, Regiomontanus's work fed into a tradition of detailed observation that, seventy years later, helped Copernicus replace Ptolemy with his sun-centred model of the solar system.

An area in which the coming of print had one of its most significant effects was in the sudden ability to categorise almost any aspect of human activity and knowledge. Print shops always had to be highly organised places, with a place for everything and everything in its place, in drawers, upper cases, lower cases and boxes galore. It was the same with the contents of books. Since it was now possible to reproduce texts page for page, and number the pages, it also became possible to give readers a quick insight into the text, both on title pages (which also allowed the printer to publicise his own creation) and in indexes. The first printed index appeared in two editions of St Augustine's *De Arte Praedicandi*, published both by Fust and Schöffer in Mainz and by Mentelin in Strasbourg in the early 1460s. By 1500 eighty-three books had alphabetical indexes.

Do not underrate the index. The index is a key to modern life, allowing access to everything from a Filofax to a national library catalogue. An index is no mere device; it may be the epitome of a book, a distillation, exhibiting insight, judgement, even creativity (for the indexer must decide on categories and subcategories, and cross-references). For that advance, printing is responsible. Before then, librarians, usually monks, had the most arcane ways of cataloguing. For one thing they had few books, few readers and no lending system, so they could store books however they wished, by size, or subject, or date of acquisition.* Such a medieval system endures today in that most brilliant and humane of collections, the London Library, where a over million books are shelved by subject, by size, and only then by letter. Entering, you become an electrical impulse in a brain, snatching at neurons. If, researching *incunabula* along its ringing metal floors and shadowy stacks, you find nothing in the Quarto section of Science and Miscellaneous – surely one of the most creative categories ever invented – then you can try Octavo, even Folio, and then fossick further in Bibliography: Printing, or Biography: Gutenberg, or History: Germany. Arthur Koestler, who suspected there was more in heaven and earth etc., claimed that once a book he didn't know he wanted *fell off the shelf* at his approach. But to find specific volumes you get down to the alphabetical index in the end.

Let the indexer take centre stage for a moment as a *major* contributor to the growth of democracy. The statutes on which English law was based were unknown to the general public until the time of John Rastell and his son William, who in the sixteenth century published every statute since

---

* In Chinese, indexes – like dictionaries and catalogues – are highly complex affairs, based on the 227 fundamental strokes used in writing characters, subdivided by the number of strokes per character (up to fourteen, or more in classical Chinese). Alternatively, each character could be number-coded, based on the 'four-corner system' which in theory provides an order for 9,999 characters. Now, with some relief, scholars have embraced the romanised version of Chinese, Pinyin.

1327. With a glance at the 'Tabula', anyone could check how many times Magna Carta had been confirmed in subsequent statutes. Monarchs and parliaments could no longer escape the fact that their rulings would be on display to any literate person, and that they or their descendants would be answerable. English law as it then evolved would hardly have been conceivable without easy access – via page numbers and indexes – to these fundamental documents.

In terms of scholarship, one measure of what was now possible emerged in the Polyglot Bible (1568–72) issued in Antwerp by the French printer and publisher Christophe Plantin (after whom the typeface was named). In his eight-volume work, Plantin published the original texts of the Old and New Testaments, using Hebrew, Greek, Latin, Aramaic and Syriac. Other polyglots followed: a ten-volume one in Paris in 1645, adding Arabic and Samaritan, and in London one of six volumes 1654–7, which added Ethiopian and Persian. All, of course, needed their own typefaces, each one adding a new dimension to oriental studies. And the whole mighty project was held together by its appendices and index.

✤✤ ✤✤ ✤✤

In Victor Hugo's *Notre-Dame de Paris*, a scholar gazes at the first printed book to come his way and stares out at the cathedral, an encyclopedia in stone and statuary and stained glass recording Christian faith and knowledge passed on from generation to generation. '*Ceci tuera cela,*' he says: 'This will kill that', the printed word will bring an end to stories in stone, and – the words imply – to received religion as passed on by priests and their artists. Hugo, speaking with the advantage of hindsight, was distilling into three words a process of fragmentation that, although under way since before Gutenberg's time, was made irreversible by the printed word.

The Church at first welcomed the power of the press as a gift of God when it was used to raise cash for a crusade against the Turks. Its blessings seemed somewhat mixed when used by opposing sides in Mainz's civil war. But the true power of what had been unleashed became apparent only in the beginnings of the vast and permanent change in European history that came to be called the Reformation. As with printing, the elements were all present – anticlericalism, corruption, the non-religious philosophies of humanism, a desire for change, resurgent nationalism, a hatred of Roman domination – lacking only a focus and a flashpoint. Wittenberg, a small town in Saxony, was the tinderbox, and Martin Luther the match.

It's a story often told, but, like Gutenberg's, there is still a mystery at its heart. It repays a close look, because these events reveal again the explosive power released when character, circumstances and technology collide. We are about to see a gear shift in the engine of revolution started by Gutenberg.

Luther was the son of a peasant miner in Saxony who made good as a foundry owner and was determined young Martin would as well. His childhood was a harsh and fearful one, haunted by witches and demons, full of obscenities and high demands. All left their impression on him. He had a talent for coarse invective, and later often spoke of being beaten by parents and teachers until the blood ran. Pop psychologists have seized on this to explain Martin's tortured character, but such treatment and beliefs were normal for rural, upright, authoritarian families in sixteenth-century Germany. For whatever reason, he grew up highly strung, easily angered and more fearful than most of a death-haunted universe in which God, the sovereign, allowed evil spirits to stalk the dark forests. He had a particular fear of storms.

Destined for law, he trained at Erfurt (in the footsteps, perhaps, of Gutenberg). It was near Erfurt, as a devout, impulsive and passionate twenty-one-year-old, that something happened to change the course of his life. He was walking a lonely road outside the village of Stotternheim when a thunderstorm broke, awakening his childhood fears. Afraid of imminent death, he cried out: 'Help, St Anne, I will become a monk!' (St Anne, the Virgin's mother, was the patron saint of miners, for in her womb she held a treasure, as the earth held treasures that miners revealed.) So, in the face of paternal anger, he vanished into an Augustinian monastery, taking his fears with him.

There he wrestled with his demons. His fears were of death, and the inexplicable mystery of life, of a universe created by an omnipotent God who had, weirdly, made a mankind mired in sin. Were we therefore damned? He could not accept that. We have been given the gift of choice, and we could choose to incline towards God, and might, perhaps, be saved. It was a big 'perhaps'. There is no bargaining with God, no way to guarantee salvation. All you could do was follow Christ and do your best. Ah, but what was that? No one can know. We are beset by paradox. If you confess you haven't done your best, you're damned; if you do, and are rightly proud of the fact, you're damned for the sin of pride. It was enough to make a man despair. But despair was a sin, and deserving of damnation. It seemed there was no avoiding purgatory, that limbo between heaven and hell in which you could endure punishments that would purge your sins. And so on, in turmoil and spiritual agony, for ten years.

Gradually, though, he fought his way, if not quite through, at least forward. It was the way of faith, which led to the bridge over the gulf of sin and death. But you could not build the bridge yourself, through force of will, or abstinence, or good works, for they only prepared the way. No one else could do it for you, either. Only God could save you. And so Luther came to his guiding principle: justification by faith alone.

If perfection was for ever out of reach, imperfections were easy to recognise. This he discovered, to his horror, when he visited Rome in 1511. He was part of a team going to plead for their monastery's continued independence. He walked all the way, was there for a month, and achieved nothing. But he saw Rome, and was appalled. Outside St Peter's, it was a clutter of decaying antiquities and malarial swamps and muggy rain. He hated the Italians (to call someone an 'Italian' was thereafter his greatest insult). They pissed in the streets. The place swarmed with prostitutes, thanks to the trade from the clergy. Pope Julius II was supposedly syphilitic and gay. The streets were full of beggars, some of them priests. Their irreverence during services made him want to vomit. Later he said he had not looked the Pope in the face, but he had looked up his arse. You can see his character in his observations: cutting, obscene, contemptuous of his fellows, driven to open a direct line to God by pessimism and incipient despair. No wonder the Church did nothing for him.

Before his trip, his monastery had received a request from the little town of Wittenberg for a professor for their town's new university, the brainchild of one of Germany's electors,

Frederick the Wise. Frederick lived in a castle, which had its own church, soon to play rather a central role in our story. To Wittenberg Luther now went, as a Bible lecturer, developing his own brand of passionate and fiercely internalised mysticism, which was independent of history, learning, the saints, miracles and those fools who thought that the empty splendours and rituals of the Church could lead to grace.

His particular horror was the market for indulgences, those bits of paper that freed you from sin. From 1476 you could buy an indulgence for a dead person and save them from further purging, and yourself from mentioning them in your prayers. In 1515 Pope Leo X, a Medici, with ambitions and a head for finance, wanted to finish a basilica over the supposed tomb of St Peter in the Vatican. To finance it, he authorised an indulgence to raise the cash. German leaders resented the flow of funds to Rome; some – notably the emperor and Mainz's young elector-archbishop, of whom more shortly – went along with it, but others balked. Among the latter was Elector Frederick the Wise of Saxony, Luther's local sovereign, who banned indulgence-sellers, thereby starting an interesting chain of events.

An enterprising indulgence-seller named Johann Tetzel now comes on the scene. Tetzel was a Dominican monk, and like many of his kind he was the medieval equivalent of a snake-oil-salesman-cum-hot-gospeller. An indulgence from Tetzel would free you from the pains of purgatory, he is supposed to have said, 'even if you raped the Virgin Mary'. Want to be forgiven for robbing a church? Nine Venetian ducats (or the same in gulden). Get away with murder? Eight ducats. Why, you could even buy indulgences that would free you of sins you had not yet committed. No need for any further suffering, beyond the pain of hearing your coins drop into Tetzel's metal-bound chest. He had been selling indulgences for the last fifteen years, couldn't afford to stop at his age (forty-eight) and saw that Saxony, now free of rivals, was his for the taking. He set up shop just over Saxony's border, in Jüterbog, a mere thirty kilometres from Wittenberg. 'Behold, you are on the raging sea of the world in storm and danger, not knowing if you will safely reach the harbour of salvation,' he bellowed at the credulous. 'You should know that all who confess and in penance put alms into the coffer, according to the counsel of the confessor, will obtain complete remission of all their sins.'

Luther, now thirty-three, was appalled. Tetzel's cynicism and materialism mocked his God, and the true nature of Christianity. He wrote later:

It was reported to me that Tetzel was preaching some cruel and terrible propositions, such as the following: He had grace and power from the Pope to offer forgiveness even if someone had slept with the Holy Virgin Mother of God . . . Furthermore, he had redeemed more souls with

his indulgences than Peter with his sermons. Further﹍
more, if anyone put money into the coffer for a soul in
purgatory, the soul would leave purgatory for heaven
in the moment one could hear the penny hit the bottom.

He did the correct thing. He wrote to his supreme spiritual
authority (excluding only the Pope), Albrecht of Branden﹍
burg, Diether's successor as the archbishop of Mainz, now
recovering from its terrible civil war of fifty years before.

He must, when he did so, have been aware that
Albrecht was not exactly the person to take his complaints
seriously. Albrecht of Brandenburg was a Hohenzollern,
the family from which the future kings of Prussia would
spring, and who were rivals to Wittenberg's Wettin rulers.
Albrecht was a plump, genial young man who loved the
good life, and already knew a thing or two about risk and
investment. He had a collection of 9,000 relics, which was
enough to save him from several million years of purgatory.
This gave him the confidence to be somewhat lax in his
moral standards. He was also remarkably ambitious.
Family connections made him archbishop of Magdeburg
when he was just twenty﹍three. A year later, in 1514, he
bought himself the archbishopric of Mainz. He was far too
young – archbishops were supposed to be at least thirty –
and it was against the law to have multiple benefices, let
alone two archbishoprics, but rules could be bent for a

price, and Pope Leo X's was not the usual 10,000 gulden, but 29,000 (think of it as £3 million; but also think a percentage of a state budget). In brief, Albrecht, a double archbishop, *Primas Germaniae*, brother of the Brandenburg elector, scion of one of Germany's most notable families, was ridiculously powerful and rich, with estates dotted over all northern Germany. His arrangement with the Pope was a sweetheart deal, which benefited everyone. His invest⁄ ment could be financed by the sale of the indulgences sanctioned by Leo for the building of his latest project in the Vatican. Leo awarded Albrecht the local franchise, agreeing to split proceeds 50–50. (He did a similar deal with Henry VIII, though in his case it was 75–25 in the Pope's favour.) With this as security, Albrecht borrowed (from the eminent Fugger banking family), paid up what the Pope demanded and stood by to receive the proceeds from his indulgence salesmen, among them the frightful Tetzel. The cash was already rolling in – some 36,000 gulden, half of which was being passed on to Rome – when Luther's letter arrived damning Tetzel and indulgences and threatening to upset the whole financial applecart.

With his letter, Luther enclosed ninety⁄five bullet points, in Latin, ostensibly 'for discussion'. It was all very proper on the surface, hedged around with humility. Luther was, after all, a nobody, a mere monk, a *fex hominum* – a shit of a man – daring to address so exalted a prelate. Imagine

Luther's feelings at adopting this stance. Exalted? A corrupt twenty-seven-year-old in bed, as it were, with a syphilitic homosexual? But one, nevertheless, who had the power to burn a little shit of a priest if he was deemed heretical. True, some of his points were explosive:

- The Pope cannot forgive sins; he can only make known and testify to God's forgiveness.
- It was stupid and wicked of priests to hand out penances for the dying to perform in purgatory.
- The Pope should know of the greed and crooked-ness of indulgence-sellers, for then he would know that St Peter's was built with the skins, bodies and bones of his flock.
- A true penitent should not whine to have his punishment lifted, but accept it, as Christ did.
- Why, if the Pope was so powerful, did he not forgive all the sins of the dead, and empty purga-tory forthwith?
- Why, since he had the money to do it, did he not build his basilica himself rather than rob the poor?

But these were only *theses*, in the original sense of 'proposi-tions' – discussion points. Luther could always take the position of the faithful servant humbly floating provocative ideas, which might or might not have value, the better to rid the Church of the unfaithful.

What happened next has been the subject of a huge debate. Traditionally, on the eve of All Saints' Day, 31 October 1517, Luther took his ninety-five 'theses' and nailed them to the door of Wittenberg's castle church, so that those entering that morning to view the relics put on show for the feast day would see them. It is a powerful image, a man hammering on a church door, driving a nail into the coffin of Catholic corruption. It was, we were told, the way one announced an academic debate. Then, suddenly, it was out of his hands. Someone copied the theses, and they were printed and flew all over Germany, leaving no one more surprised than Luther. It is a story now embedded in history books, and recalled on Wittenberg's church doors today; not the original wooden doors, which were damaged by fire in the nineteenth century, but their bronze replacements, across which the theses run in six columns.

Yet, as the late Catholic scholar Erwin Iserloh pointed out in 1961, it turns out that no one actually mentioned his action at the time. In Luther's own voluminous, self-absorbed writings — nothing. The story seems to have come from his friend, Philip Melanchthon, reformer, educator and the Reformation's future bulldog, who included it in a short biographical account after Luther's death in 1547. But that was thirty years after the event. And he was not in Wittenberg when Luther wrote his theses, arriving only in August 1518, almost a year later. Luther's most recent biographer, Richard Marius, argues that Luther would not have risked embarrassing the elector by making the theses public before they had been cleared officially for debate, which makes it seem odd that he would nail them up just where they would be seen by Frederick, right under his nose as he came to Mass that morning. In brief, the story is almost certainly a legend. Iserloh's suggestion caused outrage among Protestants unwilling to contem-plate the sudden destruction of their founding icon. The story — which after all captures an essential truth — is still reproduced as gospel.

There is one item of evidence that does not seem to have attracted expert attention. Albrecht was not in Mainz at the time. He was sixty kilometres away, in his official residence in Aschaffenburg, the other side of Frankfurt, and he did not receive Luther's letter until the end of November. Publication did not follow until after this date. Therefore, there was no copying done in Wittenberg, or the theses would have been in the public domain even before Albrecht received them. There was a printer ready and waiting locally — Johann Rhau-Grünenberg, who had been in business since 1508, drawn there by Frederick's new university — but he seemingly had no whiff of what was in the air.

Albrecht did not quite see what was coming. He asked

his experts in Mainz for their opinion. On 17 December they told him he'd better move, fast. As it happened, he had already sent the theses to the Pope a few days earlier 'in the expectation that Your Holiness will take up the matter and act, so that such an entanglement may be opposed in timely fashion, as opportunity and need arise'.

At this moment events leaped out of control. Somehow, as is the way with sensitive documents, the theses got out. Possibly, the source was one of the experts in Mainz, though it seems unlikely that any local printer (like Johann Schöffer, Peter's eldest son) would risk Albrecht's anger by publishing without permission. There are other possibilities. Luther had sent copies to a few other trusted friends, among them his immediate superior, Jerome Scultetus (Hieronymus Schultze), the bishop of Brandenburg. In any event, by mid-December enough people knew for security to be compromised. Someone, no one knows who, leaked the theses, and the dam broke with astonishing speed.

Later, Luther would claim that it was all over Germany in two weeks. Not quite; but just before Christmas – virtually the same day that Albrecht received the advice of his Mainz experts – editions of the theses, translated into German, appeared in Leipzig, Basel, Nuremberg and (almost certainly) Wittenberg itself. As suddenly, as fame comes to pop singers and football superstars today, Luther was a household name and everyone was talking about his devastating theses. The indulgences market collapsed like a popped dot com.

The noises that accompanied Luther's message of doom were probably not hammer-blows; they were the squeaks and bangs of busy printing presses.

✠   ✠   ✠

Luther was not a deliberate revolutionary. Many times he expressed shock at what he had unleashed. But the wave of publication – not only his theses but his subsequent voluminous writings – carried him forward into a storm of controversy, which made Christendom's crack into a per-manent schism.

The following year he attacked indulgences head-on as things for lazy Christians who wanted to avoid good works. Tetzel's Dominicans turned shrill in their hunt for heretics: '*Domini canes*', they were nicknamed, 'the Lord's dogs'. This only spread Luther's fame. His writings became harder-edged. What need of priests, he implied, if priests only confirmed the forgiveness God granted to the truly penitent? In Rome, prelates muttered about heresy, and in August 1518 he was summoned to answer the charges. Luther was furious. He was a loyal son of the Church. He demanded a hearing among his peers, in Germany. Rome ordered that he be bound in chains and forced to submit.

Frederick the Wise of Saxony, eager to assert his own rights, backed Luther. There would be no trip to Rome.

In October Luther went to an imperial diet in Augsburg, where an Italian cardinal, the papal legate Tommaso da Gaeta, would try to raise the astonishing sum of 800,000 gulden as German backing for an anti-Turkish crusade. He failed, not surprisingly. When Tommaso (usually known as Cajetan, after the Latinised form of his home town) finally met Luther, he was in a vile temper and ended up yelling at him to recant. Luther refused, said he would appeal to the Pope direct, and walked home seething. Cajetan demanded Luther's immediate arrest. Seventy legal briefs arrived in Wittenberg, with more orders to bind him and send him to Rome. For a moment Frederick wavered. Luther prepared to flee. Then Frederick's resolve hardened; he told Luther to stay, under his protection. If there was to be a council to resolve the matters Luther raised, it was indeed going to be a German one – a direct political challenge to the Pope, signalling a return to the dark days when Popes deferred to councils.

In June 1519 the screws tightened further, when Luther met a renowned papist, Johann Eck, in open debate in Leipzig. Pamphlets flew, crowds gathered, the rival camps as vociferous as football fans. From the start – 7 a.m. on 27 June – the two argued the issue of papal authority. Luther scored often, driving home his points that Christian authority lay with Christ and his faithful flock, not with the Pope – in effect, Nicholas of Cusa's argument from con⁄sent. For day after day, before an audience of hundreds, the two bombarded each other with erudition, passion and argument, in Latin, Eck proclaiming Luther as heretical as the Hussites, Luther striking back that at least Hussites followed their consciences, Eck claiming papal supremacy, Luther saying no, scriptures were supreme, interrupting to call Eck a liar, turning to the crowd to summarise his arguments in German. It lasted for two and a half weeks, and the two fought each other to a standstill. Luther came away thinking the Pope was the devil come in religious guise to subvert humanity. Eck advised papal condemnation.

As Rome prepared its heavy artillery, Luther fired off more salvos, with the help of the press. His sermons, tracts and polemics, all in German the better to appeal to his audience, streamed from presses by the hundreds of thou⁄sands across the land, many with his portrait (some 700 of these *Flugschriften* – 'flying writings' – have survived). He became the focus of a propaganda war of which Mainz in 1460–62 had been a tiny precedent, and a publishing phe⁄nomenon, unrivalled anywhere, ever, except perhaps by Mao's *Little Red Book* at the height of China's Cultural Revolution. At least two of Luther's sermons ran through twenty editions in two or three years. According to one estimate, a third of all books printed in Germany between

1518 and 1525 were by him. Pause to consider that figure. Of course, printing was in its infancy, but Germany at the time was turning out about a million books a year, of which a third — 300,000 — were by Luther. No comparison with the modern world stands up, but it would be the equivalent of one author selling almost 300 million books in Britain (which prints some 800 million a year), or 700 million in the US, every year, for seven years running.

Of his thunderous outpourings, perhaps the most power-ful was his *Address to the Christian Nobility of the German Nation*, a sort of Reformation manifesto. His conclusion, in German of course, was virtually a call to arms. Every Christian leader had a duty to reform the Church: 'Who-ever is guilty should suffer,' he said, and then in a righteous fury: 'Listen to this, Pope, not the all-holiest but the all-most-sinful, let God right now destroy thy seat!' Its first run was in the shops on 18 August. Within days it was sold out, to be reprinted a week later. In three weeks it sold 4,000 copies — in Wittenberg alone, where the printers became rich. In the next two years it went through thirteen editions, with pirated versions appearing in Leipzig, Strasbourg and Basel. German princes heard and took note.

By then Leo X had issued the terms of excommunication: recant in sixty days, or else. Luther's books were to be burned, and any Catholic reader of them excommunicated. Luther, naturally, did not recant. In September Eck toured

Germany, avoiding Saxony, publishing copies of the papal bull. Everywhere, it caused riots. People threatened distribu￼tors and burned their pamphlets. Luther replied with his vicious *Babylonian Captivity*, comparing Rome to Babylon and Christians to exiled and enslaved Jews, decrying the value of those sacraments not mentioned in the Bible (even marriage, which should be a union so based on love and God￼given natural urges that an impotent husband should be happy if his wife found someone else to impregnate her). Finally, he delivered the ultimate insult to the Pope, calling him a blasphemer: renounce, he demanded, 'and if you will not, we shall hold your seat as possessed and oppressed by Satan, the damned seat of Antichrist'. In Wittenberg, in a great bonfire, Luther supervised the burning of the *Canon Law*, the document that recorded the laws of the Church.

His excommunication followed in January 1521, driving Luther into a paroxysm: 'Why do we not . . . fling our￼selves with all our weapons upon these masters of perdition, these cardinals, these popes, and all this sink of Roman sodomy?'

A final confrontation was inevitable, but it could hardly be in Rome, because he wouldn't go. It would take place in Worms later that year. Violence was in the air, and Luther was nervous, fearing the fate of Jan Hus, burned when he came to Constance under the promise of imperial protec￼tion. But Luther was German, not some upstart Bohemian.

He allowed himself to be reassured and travelled under imperial safe-conduct, in a cart led by a herald and mobbed by crowds. In every town he was irked to see the imperial poster announcing to all that his books should be burned, though by now it was doubtful whose works would end up on the pyre. He could have taken heart – the posters acted as advertisements, and people who had never owned a book rushed to buy.

Worms went wild to see him. 'Nine-tenths of the people are shouting "Luther!",' recorded one of Rome's nuncios apprehensively. 'And the other tenth are shouting "Down with Rome!".' Everywhere, his publications were stacked in shops. He was the first bestseller, and a godsend for local printers (one of them, by the way, being Peter Schöffer, younger son of Gutenberg's partner and rival, and brother of Johann, back in Mainz).

On 17 April Luther stood before Charles V – a Habsburg, raised in Burgundy, ruling in Spain, and now Holy Roman Emperor – in the bishop's palace. By a window were his books, all twenty titles, which should, by papal edict, be consigned to the flames. Their titles were read. Then he was asked: 'Will you recant?' Knowing this was the moment at which the Church must formally break, he requested time. He was given twenty-four hours. When he returned the next day the room was so packed that only the emperor could sit. They wanted a simple yes or no, but he refused to comply, and to the obvious annoyance of his interrogators, he began to speak, compellingly.

There was no simple answer: he could not renounce all his books, for some were harmless. But even for his controversial books, he had a defence. His judges should beware of avoiding conflict, for sometimes the avoidance of battle preserves evil. He quoted Jesus' words: 'I come to send not peace, but the sword.' His prosecutor, Johann von der Ecken, again demanded a simple answer: yes or no. And now at last he was ready. In often-quoted words, he replied: 'My conscience is captive to the word of God. I cannot and will not recant anything, for to go against conscience is neither right nor safe.' 'Here I stand,' a later printed version interpolates at this point. 'I can do no other.' Not for the first time, print added drama to truth, so persuasively that the words now form part of Luther's memorial in Worms.

The emperor gave his reply next day. He would honour Luther's safe-conduct, but Luther was a heretic nevertheless. It was a circumspect reply, with no assertion of papal authority. Luther was allowed to stay on, for further talks, in particular with a nasty piece of work named Johannes Dobneck, a one-time peasant, now a priest and scholar, and fervid opponent of Luther and all he stood for. He threw out the scurrilous accusation that Luther was only against indulgences because he wasn't allowed to sell them himself. He made no impact on Luther, though his zeal remained undimmed, to the point that he wrote up his invective-laden views in German. Finding no friendly printer in Worms, he took off to find one elsewhere, ending in Cologne, with consequences we shall discover later.

Official circumspection was wise. Placards, signed by someone or something called Bundschuh – some peasant group, apparently – proclaimed that 400 knights stood ready to back Luther. Perhaps the lives of his accusers, perhaps the emperor's were at risk. No one knows if the knights existed, but no one was about to tempt fate.

Luther left on 26 April under imperial safe-conduct – but who knew how safe that was? Not he; nor his protector, Frederick, who wanted no risks taken, and ordered a faked kidnap. In a forest, horsemen surrounded Luther's cavalcade, seized him and galloped off with him to the castle of Wartburg, in Frederick's special care.

Back in Worms, the imperial diet declared Luther an outlaw, banned his books and forbade 'defamation'. It was a judgement that hung over Luther, and limited his freedom to move far from Wittenberg. But it wasn't going to change things. The mood remained overwhelmingly for Luther. One of his opponents, Thomas Murner, a satirist, had *Of the Great Lutheran Fool* printed in Strasbourg in 1522. 'Murner' meant 'grumbler', but was also the folk-tale name for a cat, so cartoonists across Germany portrayed him with a cat's head. Anyway, the edict of Worms had omitted to state that only papists should not be defamed, and Murner's book was seized by the local pro-Lutherite authorities.

Luther remained in hiding in Wartburg as 'Junker Georg', growing a beard and getting fat, there to begin his next work, the translation of the Bible into German. His New Testament, which took him just eleven weeks, appeared in 1522, a work of astonishing power based on the Hebrew and the Greek, vastly superior to Mentel's Latin-based efforts produced in Strasbourg sixty years before. Followed by the Old Testament in 1534, his Bible was not exactly a single-handed operation – he sought help for all languages concerned, including German – but his skill infused the project and acted as a milestone in the emergence of modern High German. He deliberately set out to escape from his own Lower Saxony dialect, aiming, as he said, 'to be understood by the people of both Upper and Lower Germany'. He avoided the purely local where he could, choosing words known across dialect boundaries, simplifying and standardising his spelling. It worked: his Bible became a model of excellence and comprehensibility, and so it remains. In linguistic influence, he was a German equivalent of both a Shakespeare and an Authorised Version.

A year later, as the Christian world went to pieces in war and rebellion, he was back in Wittenberg. The break Luther had initiated was now unstoppable. Priests started to hold services in German. Monks married (as Luther was to do four years later). His Bible set a seal on his work, speaking, as he had done, directly to the people, in ordinary language, which he continued to do, bringing calm to a city bubbling with fanaticism. He lived for another twenty-five years, long enough to see other princes seize on his ideas to strengthen their own ambitions against those of the Pope and emperor. His Reformist stream split many ways, under Zwingli in Switzerland, Calvin in France, Knox in Scotland.

After his death, a decade of war ended in 1555 with the Peace of Augsburg, which for the first time acknowledged that Germany was indeed divided between the Catholic and the Lutherans. Religious pluralism had become mainstream, or rather two main streams, the Reformist branch of which would soon divide and subdivide into a delta of Huguenots, Anabaptists, Arminians and Evangelicals, spreading into every country of Northern and Central Europe, and then across the Atlantic, in churches that shared little but their prickly independence.

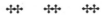

In this story, a dominant theme is the emergence of a new national sentiment. Luther addressed the 'German nation' in its own language; his appeal was to a people fed up with foreign domination; his robust language founded a cultural nationalism with dramatic and enduring political impact, though it would take four centuries to work to its logical conclusion, the creation of a nation-state. But the forces unleashed in Germany – press, language, nationalism – applied everywhere in Europe, in England as much as anywhere, with comparable consequences, and almost as much high drama.

The central figure in this act was William Tyndale. He studied at Oxford in the wake, as it were, of Wycliffe, who a century before had explored the same ground as Luther – he was anti-corruption, anti-clerical, anti-papal and a Bible translator (actually, he probably didn't do it himself, but he certainly inspired it). Tyndale was a tutor in Gloucestershire when the idea of doing a new translation dawned on him. This was in the 1520s, when he was about thirty. In 1522 he heard of Luther's translation and was inspired. In London, he asked permission to publish his own translation from Cuthbert Tunstall, the bishop of London. But Tunstall, a traditionalist utterly opposed to Luther, rejected the idea. Tyndale took off to the fount of his inspiration, Wittenberg, where his name was mentioned as a matriculant in 1524. Heady times, with the triumphant Luther just back home, keeping unruly fanatics in check, putting into practice his new teaching. The following year, Tyndale was in Cologne, the most significant centre for religious publishing, new translation in hand and knocking on the door of Peter Quentell, whose father had virtually monopolised publishing in the city after its first post-Gutenberg boom faded.

Quentell welcomed him and started work. But Cologne was no Wittenberg. Here, the old religion was still very much alive, and so was our acquaintance, Luther's luckless opponent, the embittered Johannes Dobneck, who, having fled Worms to seek a printer, had found one in the same Peter Quentell who was now at work with Tyndale. Dobneck, known by his Latin name of Cochlaeus, must have been astonished, coming from a confrontation with the satanic Luther, only to find a Lutheran protégé trying to infect his very own printer. He complained to the authorities, who obeyed the terms of the Worms edict against further dissemination of anything Lutheran and prepared to arrest Tyndale. Just in time, bearing the first ten quires of his newly printed quarto-sized sheets, he fled − to Worms, naturally.

There, he had his pages bound, the first of a printed English translation − a prologue and Matthew's Gospel (and possibly Mark's as well). The pages were then smuggled into England, to the fury of Bishop Tunstall, to whose attention they were at once brought. In Worms, the printer involved was none other than Peter Schöffer, who took on the task of printing Tyndale's whole New Testament translation. Now an expert in the art of distributing dangerous literature, Schöffer suggested a smaller trim-size than Quentell's impressive but bulky quarto sheets. Octavo volumes would be easier to smuggle. In 1526 he printed 3,000 copies of the New Testament.

Schöffer *père* had been both businessman and artist, and young Peter was even more business-minded than his father. So Tyndale's Bible is no masterpiece of printing. That was not important. It did its job brilliantly. Schöffer contacted merchants, like the wealthy Humphrey Monmouth, who arranged the smuggling. Lesser men acted as mules, unpacking the contraband and finding buyers. This was dangerous work, for discovery meant certain death for the men and their customers. Men like Robert Necton of Norwich and William Garrard of Oxford – their names known from the records of their interrogation – were burned. Monmouth himself was arrested, but proved too fat a cat to bring to trial.

The risks were willingly undertaken by a committed team. No one, it seemed, was after high profits, for Tyndale's New Testament was priced as low as possible. At a time when a hand-copied Bible cost over £30 – and when a labourer earned £2 a year – Tyndale's New Testament retailed for 4s. (20p) or less, sometimes much less. Robert Necton did a bulk deal with a Dutch importer for 300 copies at 9d. (30p), a week's wages, and well within reach of a merchant or small group of like-minded friends. By May

1526 the New Testaments were under many counters; by autumn they were sold.

Tunstall, livid, ordered as many copies as possible to be bought up and burned. Hundreds were, in a huge pyre outside Paul's Cross, a lead-covered pulpit in Old St Paul's from which papal bulls were traditionally read. Nothing could have been better calculated to help the Reformation on its way. Tyndale's Bible sold out quicker, and financed him to reprint faster – six editions, 18,000 copies, over the next three years.

He was, of course, a heretic and an outlaw, relentlessly pursued by Henry VIII's Lord Chancellor, Sir Thomas More. Despite the paradoxes in which his faith landed him, More's stern morals made him constant in his condemnation of Tyndale. It was, he said, necessary to eradicate his books – to burn them, and Tyndale himself – in order to preserve peace in the realm. Heresy was bad but tolerable, subversion intolerable. In the end More's ideology was his undoing. When his king, determined to get a male heir, set aside his Spanish wife, Catherine, and defied the Pope, Thomas stood firm for papal supremacy, and he went to the scaffold in 1535. The very same year, Tyndale, still struggling with the Old Testament, was betrayed while in the Netherlands, imprisoned for eighteen months, then strangled and burned. What madness, that an English Catholic and an English Protestant should be executed almost simultaneously for their opposing faiths.

By then Tyndale's contribution to England's tortuous and bloody passage from Catholicism to Protestantism was firmly in place. He opened the great torrent of Englishness that within a century would produce Shakespeare and the King James Version. Tyndale was England's Luther in that he used plain language. Ordinary people, he said, could not understand the Christian message 'except the scripture were plainly laid before their eyes in their mother tongue'. He is said to have told a doubting cleric: 'Ere many years I will cause a boy who driveth the plough shall know more of the scriptures than thou dost!' His lessons are with us still, or should be. In Matthew 6, the King James Version verges on the pompous: 'When ye pray, use not vain repetitions.' Tyndale doesn't mince things: 'When ye praye, bable not moche.' In I Corinthians 13, in the popular passage which in the King James contains so many puzzling references to 'charity', Tyndale uses the direct 'love', to which the New English Bible reverts. His are the tones and rhythms of the spoken word, and they, like Luther's language, anchored English-speakers in a cultural bedrock.

✠✠ ✠✠ ✠✠

Few doubted how much these momentous changes owed to the power of the press. Gutenberg, once the darling of the

Catholics, now became a Protestant hero. Printing, Luther said, was 'God's highest and extremest act of grace, whereby the business of the Gospel is driven forward', freeing Germany from the shackles of Rome, and his followers agreed. Johann Sleidan, historian, wrote in 1542: 'As if to offer proof that God has chosen to accomplish a special mission, there was invented in our land a marvellous new and subtle art, the art of printing. This opened Germany eyes, even as it is now bringing enlightenment to other countries.' A popular metaphor, echoed in many Reformation publications, compared the printing press to its forerunner, the wine press, from which poured a new and noble vintage. As John Foxe put it in his *Book of Martyrs* (1563): 'The Lord began to work for His Church not with sword and target to subdue His exalted adversary, but with printing, writing and reading . . . Either the Pope must abolish knowledge and printing or printing must at length root him out.'

The papacy, of course, had no intention of being rooted out, and fought back, using the same 'divine art', as Nicholas of Cusa had called it. In a sense, Nicholas of Cusa and Gutenberg achieved their aim in part, in that it was now possible to produce uniform texts throughout the Catholic world. But since that world was now under threat, uniformity turned into something that was rather less of a virtue – a severe conservatism, denying change.

Certain ideas that were once merely up for discussion, like Aristotelian cosmology, became fixed. Rule books on how to define sin and how sermons were to be preached issued from Rome's stern presses.

It was not enough. If some works needed to be published, others certainly didn't − a view that inspired the response that has won the Church its most scathing condemnation from non-Catholics: its attempt to control the press by banning those works of which it disapproved.

The Church had always claimed the right to approve or disapprove of books, and there had been occasional bannings, easy to impose by the Inquisition when monks produced the books for other monks. But the advent of printing raised the stakes, and the coming of the Reformation raised them higher still. In 1542, Pope Paul III set up a local branch of the Inquisition, as opposed to its fearsome Spanish counterpart, to counteract the Reformation, which it did by initiating a reign of terror that Spanish inquisitors must have envied. One of its functions was to condemn heretical books, a task paralleled in France by the Sorbonne, which published its own list of banned books. The Council of Trent (1545–63), called to retrench after the Protestant defection, established a centralised list of books that existed thanks to that *accursed* invention, printing − a list that, thanks to that *divine* invention, printing, could be distributed across the world of the faithful. Published first in 1559, the list grew year by year, and so did its malign reputation.

Actually, it was not all malign, because the *Index Librorum Prohibitorum* proclaimed what was new and interesting, and acted as good advertising for Protestant publishers. Banning never really worked: in France the official bookseller Jean André printed both the *Index* and the work of the banned heretic poet Clément Marot. Being banned was a sort of recommendation. Those on the *Index* in the early days included Peter Abelard, Lefèvre d'Etaples (the first transla-tor of the Bible into French), Boccaccio, Calvin, Dante, Erasmus, Rabelais and, of course, Luther. Eventually, there would be 4,000 books on the *Index* by the time it was disbanded in 1966.

It's easy to carp. It is the fate of censors worldwide to be reviled and ridiculed. But since the *Index* was a notorious failure – its banned authors included Voltaire, Rousseau, Gibbon, Balzac, Flaubert, Descartes and Darwin – perhaps it should not be condemned with quite the severity that should be reserved for successful censorships, of which the last century has seen a few. In its favour, as Norman Davies points out in *Europe: A History*, the Vatican saw nothing subversive about Milton's *Eikonoklastes* (banned in England in 1660) or even *Lady Chatterley's Lover* (banned in Britain from 1928 to 1960). Its inconsistencies and inadequacies seem now an admission that it was too late to do anything much about a medium that was beyond control.

This book has mostly focused on starting-points and their immediate consequences. Of later consequences there is no end, nor ever will be until paper becomes obsolete, and perhaps not then, because Gutenberg's invention introduced a change that goes deeper than any of its technical elements, singly or in combination.

When Gutenberg printed the Bible, one of his purposes was to make an object that would last as well as any scribal copy. His assumption, a universal one at the time, was that vellum was preferable to paper, because vellum was permanent, paper temporary. There are two ironies here. His paper Bibles have actually lasted pretty well. It would surely have astonished him to know that some of them are now half a millennium old. Such major works aside, paper does indeed dissolve, disastrously, but – and this is the second irony, which he would have found equally astonishing – quite often *it doesn't matter*, because now that books could be printed and reprinted it was not the material that was of significance, but the information content.

Gutenberg's invention had created the possibility of an intellectual genome, a basis of knowledge which could be passed on from generation to generation, finding expression in individual books, as the human genome is expressed in you and me, itself remaining untouched, a river of knowledge into which every new generation could tap and to which it would add, even after the last press ceases, and paper is no more, and all the vast store of accumulated knowledge is gathered in hyperspace. For there, *in perpetuo*, will be Gutenberg's Bible in all its electronic glory, to remind our children's children that this was the thing that started the revolution made by Johannes Gutenberg.

The *42-Line Bible*: A Possible Balance Sheet

DEBTS

First, the loans: Gutenberg's original 150 gulden, plus the 1,600 handed over by Fust, plus interest, plus compound interest.

Total: about 2,200 gulden.

OUTGOINGS

Gutenberg's expenditure on the Bible alone has been calculated by the German book historian Leonard Hoffmann:

Six presses:	240
Typecases and other fittings:	60
Rent for three years:	30
Heating:	20
Three hand moulds:	60
Typecasting metals:	100
Ink:	30
Paper:	400
Vellum:	300
Wages:	800
Bible (as exemplar for sales):	80
Total:	**2,120**

This just about matches the loans he had. But he was not working only on the Bible. He had another workshop to run, with several other projects in hand: the *Donatus* (a good 5,000 of those), and who knows how many of the *Sibylline Prophecies* and indulgences and other publications now lost. So we should include another (smaller) workshop, additional staff, more metal, more ink, more vellum, more paper – a *lot* more paper, because of the higher print runs. How should we cost this? As a guideline, when the monastery of St Ulrich in Augsburg established a printing office in 1472, by which time the new industry was well established and costs had dropped, the ten presses and types cost 702 gulden. So, as a back-of-the-envelope estimate, let's say he spent the amount of the original loans, another 2,200 gulden

Total outgoings: around 4,400 gulden, minimum.

INCOME

The extra costs would have to be financed by sales from the minor projects, for which estimates have to be extremely rough. A *Donatus* might have sold for half a gulden, the pamphlets and calendars for less, an indulgence for a tenth of a gulden. But each project would have been printed and sold in thousands. We could be talking of an income of 4,000+, spread over the six years 1449–55. In any event, we know that income from this source was not enough to cover costs.

For the Bible venture, we are on more solid ground. As an aid to ballpark figures, consider the following:

- a handwritten Bible of equivalent quality cost between sixty and 100 gulden;
- Gutenberg would have needed to undercut scribal copies, especially as his own would need to be rubricated and bound;
- a book printed on paper cost about a third of a vellum one.

With these and other considerations in mind, estimates suggest that the *42-Line Bible* should have yielded:

30–45 vellum copies @ 50g.:	1,500–2,250
135–150 paper copies @ 20g.:	2,700–3,000
Total:	**4,200–5,250**

THE BOTTOM LINE

So Gutenberg's rounded-out estimated balance sheet for 1449–55 might run something like this:

Costs (inc. debts):	4,500
Income received:	4,000
Income projected:	5,000
Profit in 1455:	Zero or minus
Projected profit, minimum:	4,500

German Printers Abroad:
The First Wave

TOWN	YEAR FIRST WORK PRINTED	BY
Italy		
Subiaco	1465	Sweynheym, Pannartz
Rome	1466	Han
Venice	1469	Johannes von Speyer
Foligno	1470	Numeister
Trevi	1470	Reinhard
Florence	1471	(Johannes) Petri
Milan	1471	Valdarfer
Bologna	1472–3	Wurster
Naples	1471	Riessinger
Perugia	1471	(Petrus) Petri, Nicolai
Padua	1472	Martinus
Mantua	1472	Adam
Savigliano	1473–4	Beyamus, Glim
Brescia	1474	Dalen
Genoa	1474	Scopo
Savona	1474	Bonus (Gut?)
Sant'Orso	1474	Achates, vom Rin
Vicenza	1474	Achates

Town	Year First Work Printed	By
Modena	1475	Wurster
Faenza	1476	Fer, Kandler
Trento	1476	Schindeleyp
Treviso	1476	de Hassia
Ascoli Piceno	1477	de Linis
Palermo	1476–8	Viel
Messina	1478	Alding
Soncino	1483–4	ben Israel Natan (Soncino)
Aquila	1482	Rottweil
Siena	1484	Dalen
Pescia	1485–6	Rodt
Casalmaggiore	1486	ben Israel Natan
Verona	1486	Fridenperger
Gaeta	1487	Fritag
Capua	1489	Preller
Lucca	1490	Dalen
Nozzano	1491	Heinrich (of Cologne)
Urbino	1493	Heinrich (of Cologne)
Barco	1496	ben Moses (Soncino)

France

Paris	1470	Gering, Friburger, Crantz
Albi	1475	(Anon.)
Toulouse	1476	Turner
Lyons	1477	Philippi, Reinhart
Vienne	1478	Schilling
Moûtiers	1486	Walther
(unknown)	1486	'Adam Alamanus'
Besançon	1487	Metlinger
Dôle	1489	Metlinger
Dijon	1491	Metlinger
Cluny	1492	Wenssler
Mâcon	1493	Wenssler
Perpignan	1500	Rosenbach

TOWN	YEAR FIRST WORK PRINTED	BY
French-speaking Switzerland		
Geneva	1478	Steinschaber
Rougemont	1481	Wirtzburg
Spain		
Segovia (?)	1472 (?)	'Parix'
Valencia	1473	Palmart
Barcelona	1473	Botel, vom Holz, Planck
Saragossa	1476	Botel, Hurus
Tortosa	1477	Spindeler, Brun
Lérida	1479	Botel
Tarragona	1484	Spindeler
Burgos	1485	Biel
Murcia	1487	de la Roca
Seville	1490	Paul (of Cologne), Pegnitzer, Glockner, Herbst
Salamanca	1495–7	Hutz
Orense (?)	1495 (?)	Gherlinc
Monterrey	1496	Gherlinc
Granada	1496	Penitzer
Toledo	1499	Hagenbach
Montserrat	1499	Luschner
Portugal		
Braga	1494	Gherlinc
Lisbon	1495	Nicolaus (of Saxony), Valentin
Africa		
São Tomé	1494	Valentin (of Moravia)
Netherlands		
Aalst	1474	Johannes de Westfalia
Löwen	1474	Johannes de Westfalia
Deventer	1477	Paffraet

TOWN	YEAR FIRST WORK PRINTED	BY
Utrecht	1477–8	Veldener
Kuilenburg	1483	Veldener
Delft	1497	Eckart
Antwerp	1500	Eckart
England		
London	1476	Wynkyn de Worde (Wörth)
Oxford	1478	Rood (?)
Denmark		
Odense	1482	Snell
Sweden		
Stockholm	1483	Snell
Bohemia-Moravia		
Winterberg	1484	Alakraw
Brno	1486	Stahel, Preinlein
Olmütz	1499	Preinlein
Hungary		
Budapest	1473	Hess
Poland		
Cracow	1473–4	Straube

Note: The dates record only the first *German* involvement. In many cases locals preceded them, sometimes employing German assistants. Some Germans (e.g. Achates and Wurster) set up more than one works. For details, see the source: Ferdinand Geldner, *Die Deutschen Inkunabeldrucker*, Vol. 2, Stuttgart, 1970.

Bibliography

Though the literature on the early history of printing is vast, there is no definitive, recent biography of Gutenberg in English. The best is Douglas Martin's translation of Kapr. Probably the best biography in any language at present is Bechtel's. German readers are well served by Andreas Venzke and Stephan Füssel. All of these acknowledge the primacy of Ruppel.

Febvre and Martin still provide the best history of the spread of printing post-Gutenberg. Elizabeth Eisenstein's work is a wonderful guide to its impact. The most useful summary of Gutenberg and his world is the volume published by the City of Mainz for the millennial celebrations that also coincided with Gutenberg's 600th birthday, in 2000. Janet Ing and Martin Davies provide authoritative, brief accounts of Gutenberg and the Bible. All these, except for the English version of Febvre and Martin, have excellent biographies.

The following are a selection of my main sources:

American Cusanus Society Newsletter, Long Island University, Brookville, NY.

Bechtel, Guy, *Gutenberg et l'invention de l'imprimerie*, Paris, 1992.

Bett, Henry, *Nicholas of Cusa*, London, 1932.

Blake, Norman. *Caxton: England's First Publisher*, London, 1976.

Blum, Rudolf, *Der Prozess Fust gegen Gutenberg*, Wiesbaden, 1954 (useful for the Middle High German text).

Bockenheimer, K.G., *Gutenberg-Feier in Mainz 1900: Festschrift*, Mainz, 1900.

Carter, Harry, *A View of Early Typography Up to About 1600*, Oxford, 1969.

Chappell, Warren and Robert Bringhurst, *A Short History of the Printed Word*, Vancouver, 1970, 1999.

Christianson, Gerald and Thomas Izbicki (eds.), *Nicholas of Cusa in Search of God and Wisdom: Essays in honour of Morimichi Watanabe* by the American Cusanus Society, Leiden and New York, 1991.

Colonna, Francesco, *Hypnerotomachia Poliphili*, Translated by Joscelyn Godwin, London, 1999.

Cooper, Denis, *The Art and Craft of Coinmaking*, London, 1988.

Daniell, David, *William Tyndale: A Biography*, New Haven and London, 1994.

Davies, Martin, *Aldus Manutius: Printer and Publisher of Renaissance Venice*, London, 1995.

Davies, Martin, *The Gutenberg Bible*, London, 1996.

Du Boulay, F.R.H., *Germany in the Later Middle Ages*, London, 1983.

Duggan, Mary Kay, *Politics and Text: Bringing the Liturgy to Print*, Gutenberg-Jahrbuch, Summer 2001 (pre-publication draft).

Eisenstein, Elizabeth, *The Printing Revolution in Early Modern Europe*, Cambridge, 1983 (with many reprints), abridged from her two-volume work, *The Printing Press as an Agent of Change*.

Febvre, Lucian and Henri-Jean Martin, *The Coming of the Book*. London, 1997 (from the French, *L'Apparition du Livre*, Paris, 1958).

Füssel, Stephan, *Johannes Gutenberg*, Hamburg, 1999.

Geldner, Ferdinand, *Die Deutschen Inkunabel-Drucker*, Stuttgart, 1970.

Gutenberg-Jahrbuch, Gutenberg Society, Mainz. Vital for up-to-date advances in Gutenberg research.

Hellinga, Lotte, *Caxton in Focus*, London, 1982.

Hopkins, Jasper, *A Concise Introduction to the Philosophy of Nicholas of Cusa*, Minneapolis, 1978.

Ing, Janet, *Johann Gutenberg and His Bible*, New York, 1988.

Kapr, Albert, *Johann Gutenberg: The Man and His Invention*, Aldershot (Hants), 1996. Translated by Douglas Martin. This English translation is one of those books that actually gains in translation. Kapr's original is *Johannes Gutenberg: Persönlichkeit und Leistung*, Leipzig, 1986 and Munich, 1987. This incorporates his many contributions to the Gutenberg-Jahrbuch.

Lefaivre, Liane, *Leon Battista Alberti's Hypnerotomachia Poliphili: Recognizing the Architectural Body in the Early Italian Renaissance*, Cambridge, Mass., 1997.

Mainz (City of), *Gutenberg: Man of the Millennium*, Mainz, 2000. Well-illustrated and expert abridgement in English and German of its massive Exhibition Catalogue (only in German).

McCluhan, Marshall. *The Gutenberg Galaxy*, Toronto, 1966, and often reprinted. (A non-narrative hodge-podge by turns baffling and stimulating.)

McMurtrie, Douglas, *The Gutenberg Documents*, Oxford, 1941.

Marius, Richard, *Martin Luther: The Christian Between God and Death*, Cambridge, Mass., 1999.

Moxon, Joseph, *Mechanick Exercises in the Whole Art of Printing*, ed: Herbert Davies and Harry Carter, Oxford, 1958.

Piccolomini, Aeneas Silvius (Pius II). *The Two Lovers*, Barnabe Riche Society, Ottawa, 1999. This has updated spelling. For the original spelling, see *The Goodli History of the Lady Lucres of Scene and of her Lover Eurialus,* Oxford, 1996.

Reitzel, Adam, *Die Renaissance Gutenbergs*, Mainz, 1968.

Robinson, Francis, *Islam and the Impact of Print in South Asia* in Nigel Crook (ed.), *The Transmission of Knowledge in South Asia*, Oxford, 1996.

Ruppel, Aloys, *Johannes Gutenberg: Sein Leben und sein Werk*, 1939 (and many other important contributions).

Schartl, Reinhard, *Johannes Fust und Johannes Gutenberg in zwei Verfahren vor dem Frankfurter Schöffengericht*, Gutenberg-Jahrbuch, Mainz, 2001.

Scholderer, *Johann Gutenberg: The Inventor of Printing*, London, 1963.

Seidenberger, Dr J.B., *Die Zunftkämpfe in Mainz und der Anteil der Familie Gensfleisch,* Mainz, 1900.

Sigmund, Paul, *Nicholas of Cusa and Medieval Political Thought*, Cambridge, Mass., 1963.

Smeijers, Fred, *Counterpunch*, London, 1996.

Sohn, Pow-Key, *Printing in China* and *Early Korean Printing* in Hans Widmann (ed.), *Der Gegenwärtige Stand der Gutenberg-Forschung*, Stuttgart, 1972.

Sprenger, Kai-Michael, *'voluminus tamen . . .'* (on Gutenberg's possible publication of indulgences for Nicholas of Cusa), Gutenberg-Jahrbuch, 2000.

Tyndale, William, *The New Testament*, London 2000.

Venzke, Andreas, *Johannes Gutenberg: Der Erfinder des Buchdrucks und seine Zeit*, Munich and Zurich, 1993.

Watts, Pauline Moffitt, *Nicolaus Cusanus: A Fifteenth-Century Vision of Man*, Leiden, 1982.

Wilson, Adrian, *The Making of the Nuremberg Chronicle*, Amsterdam, 1976.

Acknowledgments

My greatest debt of thanks is to James Mosley, former librarian of the St Bride Printing Library and Visiting Professor of Typography and Graphic Communications, University of Reading. His generosity, expertise, patience and wit made re-writing a joy. Thanks also to: Stephan Füssel, Institut für Buchwissenschaft, Johannes Gutenberg-Universität, Mainz, for vital help on Archbishop Albrecht and the publication of the 95 Theses; the staff of the St Bride Printing Library; Kristian Jensen and John Goldfinch at the British Library for their guidance on incunabula; Eva Hanebutt-Benz, Director of the Gutenberg Museum, Mainz; Barry Cook at the British Museum; the Koeglers at Hof Bechtermünz, Eltville; Hazel Bell for her guidance on the history of indexes; Celia Kent and Ian Marshall at Headline, who were the best of editors, and to Felicity Bryan, the best of agents; Joscelyn Godwin, Dept. of Music, Colgate University, New York, for guidance on *Hypnerotomachia Poliphili;* Don Beecher, Department of English, Carleton University, Ottawa, for his help on Piccolomini's *Two Lovers;* Nick Webb; Miyuki Nagai, University of Sheffield; Francis Robinson, Dept. of History, Royal Holloway, University of London, for his guidance on Islam; Mary Kay Duggan, Dept. of History, University of California at Berkeley, for her insights into the politics of religious publication in the mid-fifteenth century; Tahir Awan, the Muslim Directory; Morimichi Watanabe, American Cusanus Society.

Index

In the index G = Johann Gutenberg